POSTMODERN DRAMA

Contemporary Playwrights in America and Britain

Rodney Simard

UNIVERSITY
PRESS OF
AMERICA

LANHAM • NEW YORK • LONDON

Copyright © 1984 by

University Press of America,™ Inc.

4720 Boston Way
Lanham, MD 20706

3 Henrietta Street
London WC2E 8LU England

Library of Congress Cataloging in Publication Data

Simard, Rodney, 1952-
　Postmodern drama.

　"Co-published by arrangement with the American
Theatre Association"—T.p. verso.
　Bibliography: p.
　Includes index.
　　1. American drama—20th century—History and criticism.
　2. English drama—20th century—History and criticism.
　I. Title.
PS352.S57　1984　　822'.914'09　　84-15233
ISBN 0-8191-4194-1 (alk. paper)
ISBN 0-8191-4195-X (pbk. : alk. paper)

EQUUS AND SHRIVINGS, © Peter Shaffer, 1973.

All University Press of America books are produced on acid-free
paper which exceeds the minimum standards set by the National
Historical Publications and Records Commission.

For my <u>dramatis personae</u>:

Sandra Sprayberry, a Poet
Christopher Cunniff, a Physician

without whom, naught.

ACKNOWLEDGEMENTS

This study has many roots and owes many debts, none stronger than to William McClung, who began the whole process from which the compulsion behind this volume originates and continues. And to my father, Houston Simard, who has doubted the wisdom if not the sincerity of such a line of inquiry. I have an equal debt to my grandmother, Vera Simard, that can never be adequately repaid; her nurture and her home sheltered the beginnings of this project, and many others as well.

For helping me shape the basic ideas in this book, I thank my students in Contemporary Drama in the Spring of 1983, and for helping me give form to those ideas, I owe much to the staffs at the libraries at the University of Arkansas, the University of Alabama, and California State College, Bakersfield.

For the existence of this volume, my sincere thanks: to the American Theatre Association for sponsoring the manuscript; to the Research Council of California State College, Bakersfield, for their support; to Sabine Isquith, who can, and must, slay dragons; to Rainelle Sica, who accomplishes the impossible even on her birthday; to my colleagues, especially Susan Johnson, Kim and Michael Flachmann, and Peter and Barbara Grego. Their collective support and wisdom has been inestimable.

And for their kind permission for quotations: Grove Press for Tom Stoppard's Jumpers and Rosencrantz and Guildenstern Are Dead; Bantam Books, Inc., for Sam Shepard's Buried Child; and Atheneum Publishers for Peter Shaffer's Equus, copyright 1973 by Peter Shaffer.

CONTENTS

INTRODUCTION
The Need for an Aesthetic

Despite the plurality of opinions about the scope and nature of modern drama, most critics and scholars generally agree that the emergence of Samuel Beckett in the 1950s represented a turning point in traditional notions about the nature of dramatic literature. Quickly and often convincingly labeled as an absurdist, Beckett has been viewed as both the beginning and end of a tradition, simultaneously concluding one school of development and initiating another. Generally, this concept is valid, for as an experimenter, and as an Irishman living in Paris and writing in French and English, Beckett is a culmination of one modern tradition by bringing an important infusion of Continental theory to Anglo-American drama, which had long been insulated from the most significant forms of experimentalism in the twentieth-century.

From the influence of Henrik Ibsen, as transmitted by Bernard Shaw in Britain and Eugene O'Neill in America, dramatic literature in both countries had developed along roughly parallel lines, occasionally attempting experimentalism in various forms, but seldom seriously deviating from a mainstream realistic tradition. The convergence of the Anglo-American tradition of social protest and poetic drama after World War II in the mature works of Arthur Miller and Tennessee Williams in America and the new "school of anger" in Britain brought dramatic theory in both countries back to the same point of realistic focus from which it had sporadically departed since the initial impact of Ibsen in the late nineteenth-century. At this point, Beckett's Waiting for Godot appeared, and internationally, the birth of a "new" drama was heralded, the Theater of the Absurd, a concept which still dominates critical thinking, despite the emergence of an entirely new generation of dramatists whose work only tangentially adheres to the tenets of the movement as defined in Martin Esslin's study, The Theatre of the Absurd.

The problem created by trying to view contemporary dramatists as disciples of Beckett is also compounded by their refusal to abandon the realistic tradition which Beckett is often seen as refuting. Theoretically, realism seemed to stand in opposition to the European experimentalism represented by the Beckett canon, and the two forms seemed irreconcilable in scope, form, and purpose. But rather than splitting into two opposing camps, recent dramatists have risen to the challenge of this apparent paradox and have attempted a synthesis of realism and absurdism, often relying heavily on the third and less discussed major movement in modern drama, Epic Theater.

Contemporary dramatists have recognized the futility of continuing to write in a traditional realistic mode, for the appearance of absurdism clearly indicated the need for a new form of expression in a postmodern world; but at the same time, absurdism theoretically carried the seeds of its own destruction, represented by its logical culmination in Beckett. Therefore, a distinctly postmodern dramatic aesthetic has developed in response to this need for a postmodern form for dramatic expression.

Perhaps because of their ingrained realistic tradition, British and American playwrights best represent this attempt at reconciliation and synthesis, and the canons of Harold Pinter and Edward Albee both demonstrate the attempt to domesticate absurdity, borrowing extensively from the aesthetics and techniques of the other literary genres as well as bringing the concepts of Epic Theater back into the forefront of dramatic theory. Following their lead, young dramatists in Britain and America have further refined their techniques, giving substantial evidence for the emergence of a recognizable postmodern dramatic aesthetic, international in scope, but distinctly Anglo-American in form.

In the plays of Tom Stoppard, Sam Shepard, Peter Shaffer, and David Rabe, particularly, the limits and boundaries of a new concept of drama are clear. None of these playwrights offers radical breaks with established traditions, but rather a new synthetic theater, an attempt to reconcile form to meaning, philosophy to technique, in the manner of the absurdists, but without the limitations inherent in the pure experimentalism of the last generation of the modern dramatists. Adopting the methods and techniques of their predecessors without the philosophical limitation frequently seen as attendant upon them, these younger dramatists attempt to reflect a world view that characterizes their generation's concerns. Their efforts to represent accurately the postmodern world result in a new form of existential realism, wherein reality is displayed as subjective, and what may be seen as a plurality in form is actually a singularity in purpose. This sort of plurality frequently means that any discussion of drama is necessarily problematic. Granting the possible exceptions of Periclean Athens, Elizabethan England, and Neo-Classical France, many literary critics are hesitant even to recognize the genre as having an aesthetic validity equal to poetry or fiction. This question of the validity of drama is further complicated by the debasement of the literary merits of the form as a result of the popular entertainment movement of the nineteenth-century, resulting in the confusion of performance with text. In addition, scholars have tended to insist on classical measurements of form and mode with a tenacity unknown in studies in the other genres. Finally, drama has largely ignored the period boundaries established by critics of literary movements, being more closely allied to broader aesthetic developments. The result is that drama is often viewed as a step-child of literature.

The question of the validity of the genre is a fallacious one; the form exists and cannot be lightly dismissed on any grounds. It is, perhaps, the most enduring of all the arts and the basic expression of man's inherent impulse to imitate and create, thus establishing a primacy within the entire range of aesthetics.

The question of text remains problematic, for critics and scholars alike remain sharply divided on the nature of the dramatic experience. The confusion of drama with theater, which gained prominence in the last century when drama became a decadent literary form, continues to have tenacious proponents. Central to the pre-eminent theater history of Allardyce Nicoll is the inability to divorce text from performance:

Drama, . . . having one foot in the theatre, is only half a literary form, and consequently a great deal of the literary criticism which bears on the dramatic form remains either negatively inadequate or else tends to be positively distracting. [1]

Thus, the inadequacy of dramatic scholarship has long

been equated with an inherent ambiguity of the form. But a distinction must be made: theater is performance of the text within the theatrical experience wherein a dimension of significance and meaning is added through the interpretation of a playwright's work by actors; drama is the text as a literary production complete within itself. This distinction is essential, particularly in addressing the emergence of the literature of modern drama from the moribund state of nineteenth-century theatricality. As R. H. Gardner incisively observes, "Theater . . . is a frame of magic that exists outside the realm of ordinary reality. Drama occurs within it and is the principal purpose for which the frame is used." [2] Drama is the term which can be applied to a text which was created to be a self-contained unit, organic in structure and meaning, self-referential, and independent of theatrical interpretation. Drama is informed by theater but is not dependent on it for validity or existence.

Perhaps because of the pristine simplicity and brilliance of Aristotle's dramatic criticism, the standards he established continue to be the touchstones for dramatic literature. But within the context of modern drama, this approach is philosophically limiting, for as John von Szeliski notes, "producing a tragedy today which fits exact classic requirements such as the Aristotelian would really mean begetting an anachronism." [3] One of the primary reasons that modern dramatic scholars must abandon their reliance on classical concepts of form and mode is that, as Francis Fergusson notes, "Aristotle lacks our gloomy sense of the contingency of all cultural forms; he does not try to take account of the shifting perspectives of history as modern inquirers do." [4] This new perspective of history and humanity's position in time are chief characteristics of modernism (and by further extension, postmodernism) and help explain why traditional concepts of form and function are no longer operable.

"It would be possible to support the view," argues Fergusson, "that the modern theater, in its vitality and diversity, its richness or anarchy, was in fact historically derived from the break-up of that traditional theater of human action which Shakespeare could still assume." [5] In terms of form, von Szeliski observes that "the Golden Ages of tragedy were much built on man's more usual desire to base himself on the past, and our own age is the one seeming more concerned with being attuned to the future." [6] Robert W. Corrigan also observes that ours is no longer a communal world, but a collective society, post-individual and directed toward the future, not shaped by the past, and he argues that contemporary playwrights are interested in "dramatizing a condition," not in presenting an action in any Aristotelian sense. "The traditional concepts of action and character [are] artifical because they [are] incapable of expressing the essential flow and change of being," and, as manifested in the extreme of absurdism, "tragedy and comedy are both manifestations of despair, of the act which exists, exists alone in its own unmotivated isolation, unmeaningful and absurd."[7]

This over-reliance on established dicta that apply to forms appropriate to periods which have evolved both philosophically and aesthetically is the "formalistic fallacy," according to Corrigan;[8] it is the myopic insistence that one form, such as comedy or tragedy, of all ages has certain formal and structural character-istics in common. As Raymond Williams notes, "all we can take for granted is the continuity of 'tragedy' as a word."[9] Discussions of the tragic dimensions of a play such as Death of a Salesman may be interesting as intellectual exercises, but they do little to inform our knowledge of the essential nature of modern drama. The modern play must be accepted on its own terms and viewed within the framework of its own definition of the human condition, not measured against formulae inconsistent with the political, theological, economic, philosophic, and aesthetic factors of the age which produced it. Postmodern drama is essentially tragi-comedic, and as such, formalistic concepts of structure and purpose must be superseded by a concept such as the French drame, which, as defined by John Gassner, is "serious drama without tragic pretentions."[10]

In addition to the difficulties of generic termin-ology and critical approach, the notion of the continu-ity of drama has some problems unique to the genre, as well as those it shares with the other literary forms. From contemporary perspective, theatrical history is what binds traditional notions of the nature of dramatic literature. Drama is seen in the panoramic sweep of movement from pagan ritual to classical gran-deur, from the dominance of the Church in the Middle Ages to the isolation of brilliance in English Shake-spearean, Spanish Golden Age, and French Neo-Classical drama; after the relatively fallow period that extends from the late Augustan through the Romantic and

Victorian periods, drama began to resurge simultaneously around the world, giving birth to what is known
as modern drama and a variety of difficulties in dat-
ing, measurement, and definition.

Literary scholars generally agree that the modern
period began at or shortly before the turn of the
century and is characterized by a number of distinct
qualities which began to be seen as in recognizable
transformation by the end of World War II. What
follows in terms of contemporary literature is thus
often labeled as postmodern, but while current works
are distinctly different from what preceded them, no
age has not thought of itself as modern. As Tom F.
Driver observes, "we are now at a time when we can more
or less readily perceive that the period of 'modernity'
is over. It will pass into history and be given,
eventually, another name." [11] Indeed, until the passage
of time allows scholars the necessary distance to view
the sweep of nineteenth- and twentieth-century aesthetics and literature, cumbersome labels like "modern" and
"postmodern" will necessarily have to serve, although
once divorced of its psychoanalytic overtones, a term
such as "neurotic" will undoubtedly serve to characterize the period extending from the late Victorian
into at least the near future.

But in drama, even the notion of modernism is not
as well defined as in the other genres, for many
dramatic scholars would date the origins of modern
dramatic literature from Victor Hugo's preface to
Cromwell in 1827, or Georg Büchner's Danton's Death in
1835. But the landmarks of the early nineteenth-century, and earlier, must be viewed as precursors to the
more substantial and sustained achievement of Henrik
Ibsen, whose theories and productions are the first to
make a decided break with the notions of the well-made
plays established by Eugène Scribe and Victorien
Sardou. In Britain, Ibsen is without doubt the figure
immediately behind Bernard Shaw, from whose work one
can measure the beginning of a distinctly British
modern dramatic literature. However, almost thirty
years passed before Eugene O'Neill emerged to establish
a modern dramatic tradition native to America.

With the exception of the experimental forerunners,
therefore, a distinctly modernist dramatic aesthetic
dates from Ibsen, regardless of the particular nation-
ality under consideration. What Ibsen began continues
in an unbroken pattern of development through national

boundaries, from roughly 1879, the date of <u>A Doll's House</u>, through what is generally termed the modern period to the present postmodern period.

Notes

[1] <u>The Theatre and Dramatic Theory</u> (London: Harrap, 1962), p. 199.

[2] <u>The Splintered Stage: The Decline of the American Theater</u> (New York: Macmillan, 1965), p. 25.

[3] <u>Tragedy and Fear</u> (Chapel Hill: Univ. of North Carolina Press, 1971), p. 12.

[4] <u>The Idea of a Theater</u> (Princeton: Princeton Univ. Press, 1949), p. 234.

[5] Fergusson, p. 143.

[6] von Szeliski, p. 186.

[7] <u>The Theatre in Search of a Fix</u> (New York: Dell, 1974), pp. 193, 94, 205.

[8] Corrigan, p. 43.

[9] <u>Modern Tragedy</u> (Stanford: Stanford Univ. Press, 1966), p. 15.

[10] "The Possibilities and Perils of Modern Tragedy," in <u>Theatre in the Twentieth Century,</u> ed. Robert Corrigan (New York: Grove, 1963), p. 227.

[11] <u>Romantic Quest and Modern Query</u> (New York: Delacorte, 1970), p. ix.

ONE: THE CONTEXT OF THE MODERN
A New Dramatic Literature

The history of modern drama is a chronicle of experimentalism, of the emergence of a wide diversity in both structure and theme. As a matter of necessity, established forms were abandoned and traditional goals underwent a variety of metamorphoses, creating a mixture of styles and schools influenced not only by the same factors which directed the course of all modern literature, but by many of the plastic arts as well, attesting to the importance of the theatrical situation in affecting and shaping dramatic literature. Ultimately, two major movements can be seen as developing simultaneously, often in conjunction, but just as often in opposition. In addition to the various movements which are most easily dealt with as experimentalism, realism emerges as the dominant mode of modern drama, one which has continued to develop in an unbroken line from Ibsen to the postmodern playwrights, informed, shaped, and embellished by experiment, but essentially unchanged in purpose.

Victor Hugo's Cromwell (1827) can be cited as the earliest example of pre-modern dramatic realism, for life is clearly the model for the drama as its preface dictates. More important in terms of influence on later dramatists is Georg Büchner, whose first play, Danton's Death (1835), is perhaps the first significant example of naturalism in an epic form. Based on both biological and socio-economic determinism, naturalism is usually regarded as an extreme form of realism which, as a literary style, is more prevalent and effective in the novel than in drama. The first important manifestoes of naturalism came from Emile Zola, first in the preface to his dramatization of his novel Thérèse Raquin (1873), and later in Naturalism and the Theatre (1881), where for the first time the influence of modern science is fully felt and dramatic logic forcefully shifts from the deductive to the inductive.

1

The codification of this distinctly realistic thought and experimentalism came with Ibsen's fifteenth play, The Pillars of Society (1877), followed quickly by his triumphs in realistic drama with A Doll's House (1879), Ghosts (1881), and An Enemy of the People (1882), establishing him as the master of the modern realistic thesis play, simultaneously representing and exploring the problems of contemporary society. The last two decades of the century were enormously productive throughout the Western world. In Sweden, August Strindberg wrote The Father (1887) and Miss Julie (1888), the preface of which is an important statement of naturalism in the theater; in America, James A. Herne's Margaret Fleming (1890) took its place as the first native realistic drama; in Russia, the Moscow Art Theater was founded and for the first time successfully produced Anton Chekhov's The Seagull (1898); and in Britain, Bernard Shaw demonstrated his admiration of Ibsen in his critical study, The Quintessence of Ibsenism (1891), followed by his own first real success with Mrs. Warren's Profession (1893).

The effect of realism on drama was revolutionary, especially against the background from which it emerged. Due to a variety of factors, including widespread education and the rise of the middle class, the demand for popular entertainment was high throughout the nineteenth-century, but because of the patent theaters and the demands of newly-acquired cultural tastes of the public, several factors combined to produce a situation unfavorable for serious drama. Cavernous theaters, declamatory acting, star systems, and indiscriminant tastes for simple entertainment posing as cultural enlightenment lie behind the popular acclaim of the French bourgeoise melodramatic form perfected by Scribe and Sardou and imported to both the British and American stages. This type of "well-made" play is predictable in structure, conventional in message and morality, and generally contrived and mechanical, but it served to support middle class assumptions without being threatening and was widely popular throughout the century, despite the failed efforts of most of the significant literary figures of the time to change the course of dramatic convention and educate the popular audiences. What held the stages in Europe and America during most of the century was sentimental entertainment in a vaguely romantic vein and little dramatic literature was produced, although some advances were made by such dramatists as Henry Arthur Jones, Sir Arthur Wing Pinero, and Oscar

Wilde, whose inversions of the well-made play were significant in the transition from romance to realism.

The achievement of realism was to direct attention to the physical and philosophic problems of ordinary existence, both socially and psychologically. People emerge as victims of forces larger than themselves, as individuals confronted with a rapidly accelerating world. These pioneering playwrights were unafraid to present their characters as ordinary, impotent, and unable to arrive at answers to their predicaments, often vainly striving to make sense of a world where people no longer held a shared body of assumptions about the nature of existence. They were equally unafraid to be directly moralistic and didactic, striving for immediate social reform, while simultaneously attempting to represent the fragmentation of the individual's social and psychological lives. For the first time since Renaissance English and Neo-classical French drama, a body of literature emerged that directly addressed contemporary life.

The last decade of the nineteenth-century also saw the rise of the first successful attempts at experimental drama as well. In 1896, Alfred Jarry's Ubu Roi was produced to general public outrage, but nonetheless remains the first significant surrealist drama, influencing much avant-garde experimentalism after the turn of the century. In a similar attempt to represent a pre-conscious dream state, but in a more traditional structure, Strindberg produced his trilogy, To Damascus (1898), which is often considered the first expressionistic play, an early revolt against realism by one of its founders. The appearance of these two plays heralds the emergence of two of the most important experimental forms of early modern drama, the avant-garde and expressionism. The latter, in its attempts to heighten reality symbolically, became a significant form in its own right by the 1920s and contributed to the rise of Epic Theater.

The beginning of the twentieth-century saw a continuation of this same type of experimentalism, first with Strindberg's continued expressionism carried to the point of the surreal in A Dream Play (1902), and then with the cubist theoretician Guillaume Apollinaire's The Breasts of Tiresias (1903), which gave rise to the term surrealism and anticipated the theories of Antonin Artaud. In Ireland, the Abbey Theatre mounted its first production of John Millington Synge's Riders to the Sea in 1904, followed by his Playboy of the Western World in 1907, both attempting to infuse realism with the symbolic value of poetry, and introducing symbolism as a major form of early modern drama; the experiments begun at this point would be advanced by Synge, William Butler Yeats, and Sean O'Casey, culminating in the poetic drama of T. S. Eliot. In America, George Pierce Baker founded his 47 Workshop at Harvard in 1912, encouraging serious discussion of the writing of drama, which was to produce the first generation of important American dramatists; in 1925, he continued his theoretical ground-breaking by founding the Yale School of Drama.

On the continent, Jacques Copeau founded the Théâtre du Vieux-Colombier in 1913, encouraging simple and basic forms of production and incorporating many Kubuki conventions, which were to influence the important minimalist drama of the late modern period as well as to provide the direct inspiration for both the Theatre Guild of America and the Group Theatre; after his retirement in 1929, he was succeeded by his nephew, Michel Saint-Denis, who continued to be an important innovator until his death in 1949. In 1915, the first important futurist manifesto emerged from Italy, celebrating modern technology and the impersonality of the new mechanical age, and in 1916, the first dadaist manifesto originated in Zurich, announcing the nihilistic destruction of traditional art forms. Both movements were distinctly avant-garde and anticipated the emergence of absurdism at the close of the modern period.

Disillusioned during the war, Shaw began to extend his range as the master of British realism with his Heartbreak House (1913-16), infusing realism with symbolism, and beginning his period of great experimentation that was to encompass virtually all the forms that modern drama was to take. American drama also began to coalesce at this time with the establishment of both the Washington Square and Provincetown Players in 1915, who were to introduce the first significant native dramas after the close of the war. Naturalism began to diminish as a significant dramatic form during this time of theatrical experimentation, for as Frederick Lumley observes, "the anti-naturalist theatre seeks a means of creating poetic reality by extending the dramatic horizons by calling on the creative resources of the theatre."[1] In the allied art of film, the appearance of D. W. Griffith's Birth of a Nation helped point out the limits of naturalism as an effective aesthetic tool in a rapidly advancing technological world.

At the close of the war, America's dramatic promise reached fruition with the emergence of Eugene O'Neill, who established a native dramatic aesthetic that was both realistic and experimental. In 1920, he produced both the realistic Beyond the Horizon and the expressionistic Emperor Jones, which portrays the racial memories of a modern black man. Like Shaw in Britain, whose only tragedy, Saint Joan, appeared in 1923, O'Neill was a master of modern drama, working from a basis in realism, but extending into all areas of experimentalism. His naturalistic tragedy, Desire Under the Elms (1924), was followed by theatricalism in The Great God Brown (1926), and his influence on the next three decades of American drama was immediate and enormous. Following the appearance of O'Neill's work and paralleling the rapid rise of expressionism in Germany, Elmer Rice's Adding Machine (1923) explored the possibilities of expressionistic theatricality while containing pointed social criticism. Writing in this form, American dramatists were preoccupied with social concerns in the period between the wars. Clifford Odets' Waiting for Lefty (1935) and the canon of William Saroyan during 1939-41 continued this realistic tradition of the thesis play, in addition to the "Living Newspapers" sponsored by the Federal Theatre (1935-39).

Other variations on this newly developed, realistically grounded American dramatic aesthetic began to emerge as well. O'Neill's Strange Interlude (1928) shows a vigorous interest in psychology and the inner lives of characters who have become separated from their social existences. Similarly, Thornton Wilder's Our Town (1938) explores psychological states through various theatrical devices, and became, as Lumley notes, the most influential American drama on both sides of the Atlantic.[2] Lillian Hellman's drama, such as The Little Foxes (1939), anticipated the psychological realism of the 1940s, when American drama began to acquire a substantial international reputation.

In Britain, the Abbey Theatre produced Sean O'Casey's Juno and the Paycock in 1924, which continued the British attempts at achieving a national poetic drama. Advancing in poetic symbolism, Christopher Fry and T. S. Eliot both tried to write modern poetic

5

tragedy to counter the British trend of reverting to witty, drawing-room comedy, represented in such works as Noel Coward's Private Lives (1930). Eliot's poetic dramas, such as Murder in the Cathedral (1935) and The Cocktail Party (1949), were noble attempts to establish the form, but met with little popular success. The first American poetic tragedy, Maxwell Anderson's Winterset (1935), also met with popular failure; in Spain, however, Federico García Lorca, in such plays as Blood Wedding (1933), was more successful in integrating poetry with drama by concentrating on primal human conflicts.

While American drama remained realistic, exploring social issues through various forms of experimentalism, and British dramatists tried to curb the rise of ironic drawing-room satire with verse tragedy, Europeans began to extend the boundaries of modern dramatic aesthetics and form in a variety of experiments. Influenced by Luigi Chiarelli's Theater of the Grotesque, Luigi Pirandello's Six Characters in Search of an Author (1921) turns its attentions toward the intellect rather than the emotions and examines the nature of reality and illusion within the framework of the theatrical experience as a metaphor for life, clearly influencing postmodern metadrama, if not being, as Alvin B. Kernan suggests, the pivotal play in modern drama, the turning point from realism to absurdism.[3]

During the 1920s in France, a variety of playwrights were experimenting with many forms of dramatic expression. Paul Claudel used symbolism to translate his Catholicism into poetic drama; Jean Giraudoux championed a literary theater in his impressionistic dramas; and Jean Cocteau experimented in a variety of avant-garde forms, often in collaboration with Pablo Picasso, himself a playwright. Culminating the experiments of the futurists and dadaists, André Breton's First Manifesto of Surrealism appeared in 1924. In 1925, Antonin Artaud became involved with the surrealist movement, and in 1932, his manifesto, "The Theater of Cruelty," appeared. Influential on minimalist drama and the Theater of the Absurd, Artaud's Theater and its Double (1938) advocated a non-literary drama where action would take precedence over dialogue, ritual would form the basis of plot, and powerful emotions would be elicited from the subconscious of the audience; the Theater of Cruelty would be a performance in terms of the plastic and physical instead of the psychological, where things would assume the tyranny

6

they exercise over people in ordinary existence and words would become props rather than symbols. Later refined by Constantine Stanislavsky in his concept of "method" acting, these theatrical concepts of performance would come to be constructed into the literary text itself.

Experimental dramatists in Germany were also active during this period. In the 1920s, The Theater of the Bauhaus was advocating a drama of the pure movement of forms, color, and light, paralleling French and Italian efforts to reproduce a new human stature in the modern world. But perhaps the most significant German contribution to modern drama evolved from director-manager Max Reinhardt's disciple, Erwin Piscator, whose political concerns led him to develop Documentary Theater, using montages of factual materials in a didactic manner similar to the American Living Newspapers. His collaborator on many productions, Bertold Brecht, advanced these aims and techniques in his formulation of his concept of Epic Theater after his own successes in such works as In the Jungle of Cities (1923), The Threepenny Opera (1928), and Mother Courage and Her Children (1939).

Central to his concept of Epic Theater is the "alienation effect," which Brecht defines as being "a representation that creates detachment . . . which allows us to recognize its subject, but at the same time make it seem unfamiliar." Because "the new detachment is . . . designed to free socially conditioned phenomena from that stamp of familiarity which protects them against our grasp today,"[4] Brecht sought to destroy the Aristotelian sense of an audience's participation in a play by prematurely terminating scenes and frequently bringing down the curtain, using slides and other documentary materials, inserting song, and insisting that his actors remain detached from their roles. But rather than distancing his audience, he created a new intellectual aesthetic for them, forcing them to enter into the argument of his drama and winning the admiration of intellectuals and the West, contrary to his Marxist intentions.

While the 1940s were dominated by American dramatists, French writers continued their contributions. Among the experimenters, Jean Anouilh achieved his first world success with his Antigone in 1943, and in the following year, Jean-Paul Sartre's No Exit was tremendously influential, despite its conventional structure, for his direct application of existential philosophy and his development of littérature engagée. Sartre introduced the ideas which were to bring modern drama to its logical conclusions and to suggest the foundations for a postmodern dramatic aesthetic.

Establishing America's place in world drama, Arthur Miller's Death of a Salesman (1949) represents the logical culmination of the native realistic social drama, using expressionistic techniques to infuse the play with tragic proportions. Similarly, Tennessee Williams' The Glass Menagerie (1945) and A Streetcar Named Desire (1947) are realistic dramas with poetic techniques used to focus on the essential loneliness of the individual. Grounded in realism, but modified with experimental devices, the works of both dramatists reflect the concerns of existential philosophy in their subject matter without yet reflectng those same philosophic concerns in form.

Form and function approach unity, however, in 1950, when Eugène Ionesco's first play, The Bald Soprano, was produced and the shape of modern drama first represented its content, launching the Theater of the Absurd. An attempt to reproduce in structure the clichéd lack of communication between people and the fragmentary, chaotic nature of modern existence, Ionesco's drama soon had many rivals. Arthur Adamov's Ping Pong (1955) presents pinball machines as metaphors for life in a parodic account of the search for meaning in life. In The Balcony (1956), Jean Genet presents life as a series of brothel fantasies fulfilled against a background of revolution and destruction. But the triumph of absurdism also appeared in English in 1956; Samuel Beckett's Waiting for Godot, a minimalist drama in two balanced acts, imagistically functions as a metaphor for the individual's stasis and inefficacy in discovering a purpose to existence.

In many ways, absurdism represents the full maturity of most experimental techniques and avant-garde purposes. As Martin Esslin argues, "The Theatre of the Absurd has renounced arguing about the absurdity of the human condition; it merely presents it in being --that is, in terms of concrete stage images."[5] It is an embodiment of existential philosophy rather than a display of it, as is the drama of Sartre and Albert Camus; it becomes an existential artifact. Theater of the Absurd is a total abandoment of superficial realism in order to convey the anxieties and working of the mind, aiming at "expressing an intuition in depth" which should be "apprehended in a single moment" but is forced to unfold.[6] Edward Albee describes the movement as:

an absorption-in-art of certain existentialist and postexistentialist philosophical concepts having to do, in the main, with man's attempts to make sense of himself out of his senseless position in a world which makes no sense--which makes no sense because the moral, religious, political and social structures man has erected to "illusion" himself have collapsed.[7]

In this mode, structure, staging, and character are reduced to their smallest possible working components in an attempt to correspondingly maximize meaning.

Just as absurdism reduced realism to a philosophic concept, a new version of realism surfaced from the hibernating British drama. Also in 1956, the year of the English translation of Godot and the same year that O'Neill's posthumous Long Day's Journey into Night was produced in America, John Osborne's Look Back in Anger opened. A thoroughly realistic play conventionally structured, it extended the boundaries of both dramatic language and material. This new representative of the Theater of Anger by a "new wave" dramatist directly confronted the harsh realities of ordinary life, celebrating the common and employing the language of revolution. New voices of the proletarians emerged from the working class: Brendan Behan, Arnold Wesker, and Shelagh Delaney, among others.

At the end of the modern period of drama, therefore, two distinct strands emerged. Experimentalism had coalesced and achieved a culmination in absurdism, while realism had dropped theatrical trappings and ceased experiment in expressionism and poetry, achieving a clarity and directness of purpose it had not possessed since its inception. The postmodern dramatist rises to the challenge of the two apparent culde-sacs to unite seeming opposites into a new and unified dramatic aesthetic.

The initial impression one may receive from this historical overview of the emergence of modern drama to its fruition in the 1950s is of diversity and fragmentation, and to the extent that the early twentieth-century was a period of intense experimentalism, this may be an accurate assessment. In terms of the continuity of purpose and the range of concerns, however, the

period can be viewed as the attempt to codify a substantial and recognizable dramatic aesthetic.   The
emergence of modern drama as both a form and a movement
was in direct response to a need to dramatically confront and represent a new human existence. As people
began to view themselves as moderns, rather than simply
being modern in the generic sense, their needs for
tools to interpret their confrontation with a distinctly modern reality began to assert themselves in
all the arts.   Inherent in the dramatic form is the
dialectic between illusion and reality, the attempt to
explore the illusions that cloak an essential reality
and to arrive at a distinction between what is true and
false.

The rise of empiricism demanded that all the arts
confront existence in a realistic manner. Drama first
responded to this need with naturalism, an attempt to
express the physical sources and limits of the individual's newly acquired position in terms, chiefly, of
heredity and environment, replacing metaphysics as the
source of an inability to determine one's own destiny.
However, as Joseph Chiari observes, naturalism "denies
the existence of any active informing substance and
reduces the world to material elements, therefore it is
an exact description of material elements."[8]   In its
failure to expose either a subjective or objective
reality, it came to be viewed as a "colorless, behav-
iorist idiom,"[9] which more accurately reflected the
methods rather than the results of science. Naturalism
was a tool to represent surfaces, which, rather than
being the reality, were seen to be illusions.   Surface
realism was an important stage in the full concept of
realism, but reality, as people increasingly strove to
explore, was deeper, inaccessible to the inductive
reasoning of the laboratory.

Nonetheless, modern drama was established in a
realistic vein and continued to be faithful to immediate action verifiable by experience. Dramatic literature reflected a concern with characters and the social
consequences of their actions, both internal and
external. As a result, psychology became an essential
tool of the dramatist and many experimental techniques
were advanced that facilitated this depiction of
characters' inner lives, their subjective reality.
What was to happen to the dramatic mode or form during
the modern period was not a series of departures from
realism and returns to it, but rather a series of
refinements and variations on the thesis or problem

play advanced by Shaw under the influence of Ibsen. Within the Shaw canon, this process of refinement and experimentation is easily discernible. In his movement from the social attack of Mrs. Warren's Profession to the Nietzschian surrealism of Man and Superman to the symbolism of Heartbreak House to the tragedic vision of Saint Joan to the essential absurdity of Too True To Be Good, he demonstrates his commitment to exploring basic realities, whether embodied in social issues or in his characters' psyches. These plays are elements of a unified vision, not the product of fragmentation, and as Joseph Wood Krutch observes, "though he never wrote it all down in systematic form, Shaw has at one time or another propounded the parts of what is probably the most inclusive body of doctrine since Thomas Aquinas."[10] Monolithic in terms of theatrical influence, Shaw is also the master of modern British and American dramatic literature by his concern with text, his elaborate stage directions, and introductory essays on diverse social and philosophic issues.

Because the American tradition is also the British tradition, Shaw's first important disciple is O'Neill, whose canon demonstrates the same comprehensive view and fertile diversity. Starting from the basic realism of Beyond the Horizon, he moved to expressionism in The Emperor Jones and The Hairy Ape to naturalism in Desire Under the Elms to surrealism and symbolism in Strange Interlude and The Great God Brown, and back to realism in The Iceman Cometh and Long Day's Journey Into Night. Like Shaw, O'Neill established a body of modern dramatic literature on his side of the Atlantic, and together, the two dramatists represent the fountainhead of a realistic Anglo-American dramatic aesthetic.

Ruby Cohn argues that beneath the surface realism in the works of Shaw and O'Neill, the "plays contain the prototypical Existential confrontation--man vs. his own mortality."[11] This attempt to render existential realism in dramatic form lies beneath all experimentation that follows in the course of development of modern drama in Britain and America. Essentially Continental in nature, modes such as surrealism, symbolism, dadaism, and futurism never appear in pure form in Anglo-American drama but are informing techniques aimed at further revealing inner realities and heightening the effect of psychological exploration, as in Shaw and O'Neill. What is often labeled theatricalism is most often a combination of these experimental forms, where the various resources of the theater are exploited to highlight realistic dramatic conventions. While theatricalism may be viewed as a sustained technique in such a work as Wilder's Our Town, its use is usually isolated, such as O'Neill's use of masks in The Great God Brown or Shaw's "Don Juan in Hell" segment in Man and Superman.

The thirty years that separate the two fathers of modern drama were represented in the discrepancy between what their immediate followers were trying to accomplish in Britain and America. Efforts by the founders of the Abbey Theatre, and later by such playwrights as Fry and Eliot, to establish a native poetic drama were incompatible with the modern insistence on realism, and their neo-romantic efforts met with little success. However, their theories would be incorporated into the two most significant rivals of dramatic realism, Epic and Absurd theater, which were to inherit elements of verse in the forms of alienation and lyrical language, respectively. While the British experimented in verse in the period between the wars, American dramatists continued to explore the limits of realism in an unbroken line from O'Neill. Social issues in realistic modes were the sole concerns of the second generation of Americans. Wilder, Odets, Hellman, Saroyan, and William Inge all followed O'Neill by modifying realism with a variety of theatrical devices which evidence less concern for text and more for performance.

Despite the range of Continental experimentalism, Anglo-American drama remained faithful to the realistic tradition of the thesis play for the first half of the century. The appearances of Miller and Williams and the international acceptance they received mark the period of maturity for American drama, a point not reached in Britain for another decade until the appearance of Osborne and the school of anger. As Robert Brustein was able to remark as late as 1969, "the whole development of recent English drama inspires an American with a sense of déjà vu."[12] But by the mid-1950s, Anglo-American drama stood in real danger of growing moribund from a lack of experimentalism, attested to by the critical attention received by such a play as Look Back in Anger; a thesis play conventionally structured and concerned with realistic social issues, Osborne's work was heralded as revolutionary for abandoning experimentalism. The experimental techniques which had influenced Anglo-American drama since Shaw had ceased to be experimental against what was being attempted on the Continent. The time was right for the appearance of Samuel Beckett, an Irishman writing in French, who would bring an infusion of Continental theory to the realistic tradition.

Even before Beckett's sensation with <u>Waiting for Godot</u> and the arrival of Theater of the Absurd, another important dramatic movement had established its tenets and reached an inchoate maturity, largely unheralded in major theoretical schools: Epic Theater. Derived from expressionism, the attempt to symbolically heighten reality through a series of theatrical images, or, as Alvin B. Kernan argues, "the style in which the artist dispenses with probability in order to express directly his sense of life in images,"[13] Epic Theater received full expression in the works of Brecht. But epic techniques were to influence modern drama only tangentially; the postmodern playwrights were to look back to the epic as one means of reconciling the opposition they perceived between realism and absurdity.

Notes

[1] <u>New Trends in Twentieth Century Drama</u>, 4th ed. (New York: Oxford Univ. Press, 1972), p. 14.

[2] Lumley, p. 333.

[3] "The Attempted Dance: A Discussion of the Modern Theater," in <u>The Modern American Theater</u>, ed. Alvin B. Kernan (Englewood Cliffs, NJ: Prentice-Hall, 1967), p. 26.

[4] "A Short Organum for the Theatre," in <u>Playwrights on Playwriting</u>, ed. Toby Cole (New York: Hill & Wang, 1960), p. 88.

[5] <u>The Theatre of the Absurd</u>, revised updated ed. (Garden City, NY: Doubleday, 1973), p. 6.

[6] Esslin, p. 355; italics in original.

[7] Quoted in John Killinger, <u>World in Collapse: The Vision of Absurd Drama</u> (New York: Dell, 1971), pp. 2-3.

[8] <u>Landmarks of Contemporary Drama</u> (London: Herbert Junkins, 1965), p. 31.

[9] Laurence Kitchin, <u>Drama in the Sixties</u> (London: Faber and Faber, 1966), p. 99.

[10] "Modernism" in <u>Modern Drama</u> (Ithaca, NY: Cornell Univ. Press, 1969), p. 3.

[11] _Currents in Contemporary Drama_ (Bloomington: Indiana Univ. Press, 1969), p. 3.

[12] _The Third Theatre_ (New York: Knopf, 1969), p. 129.

[13] Kernan, p. 26.

TWO: SAMUEL BECKETT
The Last of the Moderns

As an absurdist, Samuel Beckett is both representative of and superior to the movement, but the ways in which he is most closely allied with the Theater of the Absurd are those which most clearly exhibit the value of the particular mode. As Martin Esslin argues, "The Theatre of the Absurd . . . can be seen as the reflection of what seems the attitude most genuinely representative of our own time [1973]" and its contribution to dramatic art.[1] This contribution is most often characterized by an abandonment of the traditional devices of discursive thought, a simultaneous devaluation and elevation of language arising from a basic mistrust of its expressive potential, a presentation of characters who are embodiments of basic human attitudes, and a structure based on the circularity of universal situations rather than specific events. In these ways, absurdism is clearly a culmination of many of the experimental techniques in evidence for almost a century.

Esslin's observation that the writers who comprise absurdism form no organized school, share no unified aesthetic, is reflected in a comparison of Beckett with a dramatist such as Eugène Ionesco, whose works more clearly fit the mechanical definitions of absurdism. An absurdist play is one in which the absurdity of existence is demonstrated by the text itself; no argument is posited, but rather the work stands as an example of absurdity in both form and content, which are often indistinguishable. In such a play as The Bald Soprano, the characters are bourgeoise stereotypes, their dialogue clichéd and pointless, and the action defies any cause and effect analysis. The meaning of the play is reflected in the meaninglessness of the content, and the philosophical implications of the play are derived from the total impression one receives from having experienced it. This makes for excellent theater in its best manifestations but lacks

15

the dramatic dimension demanded for consideration as important literature. Thus, Ionesco's drama is that which most truly exhibits the aims of absurdism as a movement and the cul-de-sac it represents. Beckett's drama is far more suggestive, refusing to admit the boundaries recognized by the absurdist techniques. The difference between the two writers is, as Joseph Chiari observes, that "the world of Beckett is only absurd and meaningless because of the absence of Godot. That of Ionesco is just plain incoherent, mechanical and riddled with fantasies and nightmares, and lacking a centre which is the self-awareness of absence."[2]

Proceeding from, rather than abandoning, traditional Western dramatic forms, Beckett "gave the theatre a new point of beginning," according to Hugh Kenner, by this distrust of expansion and by returning to basics.[3] In response to the same existential philosophy which collectively inspires all the absurdists, Beckett also finds art as an imitation of external nature unsatisfactory and attempts to communicate a totality of perception and an intuition of being; as Esslin observes, "the existential experience is . . . felt as a succession of attempts to give shape to the void" that many modern playwrights feel is the essence of existence.[4] When Ruby Cohn notes that "although Beckett has been confused with the philosophically existential, he has moved ever closer to the essential,"[5] she points out both the value and limitations of his work. While offering "concentrated imitations of the actions of our lives,"[6] Beckett's plays "constitute the culmination of existential thought itself, precisely because they are free of any abstract concepts or general ideas, and thus escape the inner contradiction of existentialist statements that are couched in the form of generalizations," which, according to Esslin, makes them superior to discursive plays such as Sartre's, which are "denied the profound immediate experiential validity of Beckett's writings."[7] But while akin to the experiential dimension of most absurdist drama, Beckett's canon embodies both a technique and an aesthetic which serve as the foundations for a postmodern approach to dramatic expression as the succeeding generation of playwrights attempts to avoid the limitations built into his work.

Beckett's methods are well documented both in relation to absurdism and by themselves and are founded on a particular set of assumptions that exemplify the best of the Theater of the Absurd. The notion of time, which Beckett approaches through his study of Proust, is no longer meaningful as linear, sequential, and cumulative, but is seen as relative and subjective. This view of time linked to the concept of circular structure recalls Marshall McLuhan's observation that the modern medium is the message, and in Beckett, the combined effect is "polyphonic," [8] a simultaneous interaction of elements rather than a linear plot development. This subjectivity is what Thomas R. Whitaker observes to be "the modern theme," "the consciousness of the consciousness. As our late romanticism gives another twist to the baroque, every point of view tends to include an insistence that it is only a point of view. Every medium becomes its own most important subject." [9] But Beckett is not content with this effect as are many of his contemporaries, such as Ionesco. Philosophically, his plays suggest a questioning of the subjectivity of the reality that lies behind any experience, in effect, a probing of the nature of reality.

John Fletcher and John Spurling observe that "the repeated attempts at formal innovation in the theatre have been directed at obtaining more reality, not less," [10] as some critics have erroneously observed in the intentions of the absurdists, and in this expansion of reality lies one of Beckett's most important contributions to dramatic practice. If Chiari's observation that "art is the symbolic equivalence of an individual self-consciousness apprehending itself in the act of being self-conscious" is accepted, then such a work as Godot must be seen as "a striking example of the dramatic embodiment of true realism in which every aspect of phenomenal appearance is informed with substance and is symbolic of true reality." [11] The reality Beckett portrays emerges from his and his characters' own subjectivity, expanding the notion of reality to include internal as well as external reality.

By suggesting that reality is valid only in perception, that it is an internal quality, without resorting to the traditional psychoanalytical tools, Beckett's drama evokes the universal rather than the particular, freeing his characters from the limits of time and space while suggesting the subjective and universal nature of all experience. As Alec Reid notes, such a play as Godot cannot have a single definitive meaning which would exclude all others, for Beckett's plays are essentially imagistic, simultaneously specific and metaphoric. [12] The absurdist's aim is not to strip metaphysics from technique to create chaos, but an attempt to construct a harmonious flow of images with manifold ramifications of meaning.

The technique whereby this universality is achieved employs many devices from experimental drama while calling on a variety of theatrical conventions. In his texts, Beckett demands that the stage be as bare as possible, countering the necessary illusion of specific place inherent in theatrical performance, with as few specific trappings as possible, ranging from the road and tree of Godot to the nothingness that surrounds Mouth in Not I; place could be at any tree beside any road or anyone's mouth while simultaneously being located in the two precise locales where the actions-- or nonactions--of the two plays occur. Stage proper- ties are similarly only the most essential and the most common. But while the ashcans of Endgame are over- whelmingly ordinary, they contain Nell and Nagg, a particularly suggestive and subjective function. Beckett's point in using these ashcans is to create an image, one which functions quite concretely in his play as well as ranging in philosophical universality. The cans are not simply a symbol of the modern attitude toward the aging, or a warning about nuclear holocaust, or a symbol of the artistic necessity of discarding the past, or representative of man's inhumanity, or any of the ramifications they suggest; they are all these evocations and more, while still being two specific stage props. Beckett asks his audience to accept the ashcans for nothing more than what they literally appear to be, while figuratively their presence sug- gests incalculable subjective interpretations. In this way, things are represented as both the trappings of ordinary existence and the symbols of human uses of them. The power that things exercise over people in existence is suggested in a poetic image, complete within itself as presented in the text, while richly evocative within a range of subjective experience.

Plot in Beckett is often considered static, but what Beckett dramatizes are people in the process of self-perception, surrounded by the minimal trappings of existence. Characters reduced to their lowest common denominator, from the tramps of Godot to the lips of Not I, contemplate the nature of their existence in the present, at a given moment in time, located subjec- tively within their individual perceptions of a time continuum in a reality located in the psyche. It has become a commonplace that his characters are not men, but modern man, contemplating his own modernity, per-

18

ceiving his existence while struggling to define his essence. His plays both portray and are moments of existential awareness. Thus, questions about the identity of Godot are moot, for the process of waiting, of perceiving and being in time, is the subject of a play that is irreducible to formulaic interpretations.

Having neither the dark vision of Genet's plays nor the essential playfulness of Ionesco's theater, Beckett's drama is philosophically more profound, and as evidenced by his development as a dramatist, it is self-completing; his philosophical orientation cannot be further developed in the works of another play-wright. Thus, thematically Beckett is his own furthest logical extension. Critics disagree, however, about the nature of Beckett's dramatic vision. George Well-warth maintains that "the main point of the criticism is that Beckett could not possibly mean what he appears to mean because that would be very unpleasant indeed," and that "Beckett is the prophet of negation and sterility. He holds out no hope to humanity, only a picture of unrelieved blackness; and those who profess to see in Beckett signs of a Christian approach or signs of compassion are simply refusing to see what is there."[13] Despite the pervasiveness of this evalua-tion, an assessment such as David H. Helsa's is more accurate:

> Beckett is the prophet of the mess, the prophet of the absolute absence of the Absolute. If he holds out any hope at all for the human experi-ment, it is a hope founded on man's capacity to endure a world in which the light is dying, the temperature is dropping, meaning has long since dissipated, and existence is a painful slogging from station to station of a Via Dolorosa that has no telos but merely a terminus.[14]

Beckett's movement from the dramatic fertility inherent in Godot and Endgame, whatever their philosophical overtones, to the dramatization of that philosophy in the anguish of the individual soul in Not I and Breath, seems to represent the logical extension of his own pessimistic if not nihilistic vision. Indeed, his experiments in mime increasingly suggest that he may abandon the dramatic for the theatrical entirely.

Despite their concepts of dramatic vision, their developmental limits are not necessarily inherent in the absurdists' actual methods, and their followers have been able to assume their methods while rejecting their philosophical positions. The minimalist tech-niques of the absurdists are adaptable, however, only up to a certain point. For example, the minimalistic staging, insistence on inner realities, use of the poetic language of monodrama, and presentation of symbolic plot are the devices the absurdists use to achieve their primary effects. The aim of the absurdist method is to draw the reader into the action, not in the Aristotelian sense of engagement, but by presenting subjective conscious states that force readers to react subjectively themselves, engaging them in a psychological reality presented, rather than argued, in terms of the poetic image. But this distrust of discourse and traditional methods of expansion can result in two extreme positions which both defeat the dramatic aims of absurdism. The play can become completely self-referential and a philosophic artifact, as do many of the plays of Ionesco, or it can become a purely theatrical experience, as such works as Beckett's Not I approach. The dramatic effect in either case tends to be emotional to the point of excluding the intellect; one reacts without involvement in a way similar in effect but opposite in intention to the alienation effect in Brecht's Epic Theater. Beckett, however, like all the absurdists, ceases to have a significant influence on postmodern drama when he moves from the existential to the essential, from an affirmation to a negation of the dramatic form.

Suggested in this movement toward reduction is the concept of cruelty propounded by Antonin Artaud. In the attempt to evoke strong emotion, to attempt to change the course of the audience's lives, Artaud proposed a ritualized drama that called on employing the resources of the theater to their fullest extent, emphasizing performance over text. By exhibiting a distrust of language to the point of abandoning it, relying on the theater rather than on his drama, and creating a visual retreat into pure metaphor, Beckett loses his influence on the succeeding generation of dramatists who reject the nihilism of the form while respecting the purity of its intention. Under the influence of Artaud, drama and dramatic literature cannot easily coexist.

A consideration of Beckett and his contribution to absurdism, however, does not complete a consideration of modernism, for in Brecht's work, another important dramatic theory was paralleling the rise of absurdism. In his reconsideration of his often misunderstood labeling of the Theater of the Absurd, Esslin concludes:

What I feel is that the writers I have grouped in that category have developed a whole new vocabulary of theatrical forms that has enriched the stage's possibilities of expression immensely and added a new dimension to the art of the theatre. The innovations and new devices introduced by the absurdists will, I am convinced, continue to be used and will eventually be absorbed into the mainstream of the tradition . . . . Above all they have demonstrated that poetry in the theatre is not merely a matter of language but that the theatre itself is a form of poetry: concretized metaphor, complex imagery on multiple planes of meaning and association, from the most earthily concrete to the most esoterically abstract. . . . The absurdists have further demonstrated the theatre's ability to deal not only with external reality in providing a concrete and photographically correct reconstruction of real life but also, and much more interestingly, with the vast field of internal reality--the fantasies, dreams, hallucinations, secret longings, and fears of mankind.

Rightfully distinguishing between realism and the experimental, except in the context of British anger, Esslin also identifies "just two main spearheads of today's [1969's] avant garde: a socially committed, left-wing epic theatre on the one hand, and an introspective, non-political, grotesque drama on the other," perceptively pointing to another significant event of 1956, the first visit of the Berliner Ensemble to Britain, only weeks after Brecht's death. Continuing in his analysis of contemporary experimentalism, Esslin contends that "far from being contradictory and mutually exclusive methods, these two styles are complementary and could well be fused in the futrue. And it is here that I see at least a possibility for a new and exciting step forward for the avant garde of drama." [15]

This synthesis that Esslin prophesied in 1969 has largely been realized, although not quite in the form he suggested. Epic Theater, whose basic tenets were formulated in the 1930s, has been seized upon by the postmodern playwrights as one means of reconciling the advances made by the absurdists to an essentially realistic Anglo-American dramatic tradition. Perhaps the delay in influence of Brecht's ideas on the Anglo-American theater can be attributed to the general atmosphere of the World War II era and its general anti-German bias, as well as Britain's obvious dramatic insularity and the pervasiveness of McCarthyism in America.

Many of Brecht's techniques have been borrowed by contemporary dramatists, and in its experimental na-

21

ture, the concept of the epic shares many similarities with absurdism. Brecht's statement that the theater "must amaze its public, and it achieves this by a technique of making the familiar seem strange," is distinctly analogous to the techniques of the Theater of the Absurd. Similarly, his plea for a concept of total theater resembles the later manifestations of absurdity:

> So let us invite all the sister arts of the drama, not in order to create an "integrated work of art" (Gesamtkunstwerk) in which they all offer themselves up and are lost, but so that together with the drama they may further the common task in their different ways; and their relations with one another consist in this: that they lead to mutual detachment.

This detachment is central to epic thinking, the distanciation or alienation effect that achieves much the same effect as the extended visual metaphors of the late Beckett canon. As a technique, alienation is aimed at consciously inserting an intellectual element into drama, forcing readers--or in the case of this highly theatrical mode, audience--into thinking, judging for themselves from the variety of materials presented within the framework of the drama. Also, Brecht's warning that "stylization should not remove the natural element but should heighten it"[16] is parallel to the absurdists' attempts to expand the definitions and boundaries of dramatic reality beyond the limits imposed by naturalism.

The similarities between the two modes are misleading, however, if they are viewed as originating from the same sources, rather than from the same motive--to supersede traditional realism. Epic techniques are complementary to those of absurdism, and thus tend to offer alternatives to the logical self-fulfillment reached by absurdist methods, alternatives which are not necessarily more effective in themselves, but which tend to avoid structural and philosophic finality by their very opposition. Techniques such as symbolic or expressionistic heightening of detail for emphasis, shifts in tone, insertion of music or objective commentary, as well as the non-participatory, objective acting style advocated by the proponents of the epic, all serve to destroy reader/audience identification and have the effect of forcing subjective interpretation, but the aims of the two modes remain quite incompatible in theory. While absurdism achieves an immediacy, an involvement of the reader in the very consciousness of the character and is subjective in both form and

22

effect, epic strives for alienation, emphasizing external qualities in a social and didactic context. Nonetheless, both aims find expression in the attempts of postmodern dramatists attempting to explore the nature of a distinctly existential reality.

Attempts at this synthesis appear as early as the works of some of the school of anger. Brendan Behan's use of music and comic objectivity in The Hostage (1959) and Osborne's satirical musical, The World of Paul Slickey (1959), represent success and failure at epic detachment, while Osborne's Luther (1961) and Robert Bolt's A Man for All Seasons (1960) are both epic in intent. But a truly successful synthesis of both absurdist and epic methods with realism and the emergence of a recognizable postmodern dramatic aesthetic, wherein realism and experimentalism effectively coalesce, can be dated from the first appearance of Harold Pinter and Edward Albee.

Notes

[1] The Theatre of the Absurd, revised updated ed. (Garden City, NY: Doubleday, 1973), p. 4.

[2] Landmarks of Contemporary Drama (London: Herbert Junkins, 1965), p. 76; Laurence Kitchin, Drama in the Sixties (London: Faber and Faber, 1966), p. 31, shares much the same opinion.

[3] A Reader's Guide to Samuel Beckett (New York: Farrar, Straus and Giroux, 1973), p. 13.

[4] Introduction, Samuel Beckett: A Collection of Critical Essays (Englewood Cliffs, NJ: Prentice-Hall, 1965), p. 9.

[5] Just Play: Beckett's Theater (Princeton: Princeton Univ. Press, 1980), p. 13.

[6] Ruby Cohn, Back to Beckett (Princeton: Princeton Univ. Press, 1973), p. 216.

[7] Esslin, Beckett, p. 5; italics in original.

[8] Esslin, Absurd, p. 25.

[9] Fields of Play in Modern Drama (Princeton: Princeton Univ. Press, 1977), p. 12.

[10] Beckett: A Study of His Plays (New York: Hill and Wang, 1972), p. 21.

23

[11] Chiari, pp. 25, 71-72.

[12] "From Beginning to Date: Some Thoughts on the Plays of Samuel Beckett," in Samuel Beckett: A Collection of Criticism, ed. Ruby Cohn (New York: McGraw-Hill, 1975), p. 64.

[13] The Theater of Protest and Paradox (New York: New York Univ. Press, 1964), pp. 37, 51.

[14] The Shape of Chaos: An Interpretation of the Art of Samuel Beckett (Minneapolis: Univ. of Minnesota Press, 1971), p. 165.

[15] Reflections: Essays on Modern Theatre (Garden City, NY: Doubleday, 1969), pp. 185-87, 193, 195.

[16] "A Short Organum for the Theatre," in Playwrights on Playwriting, ed. Toby Cole (New York: Hill and Wang, 1960), pp. 89, 104, 103.

THREE: HAROLD PINTER & EDWARD ALBEE
The First Postmoderns

First appearing in 1957, Harold Pinter's work falls chronologically into the new wave movement, or the school of anger, and while his biography supports an inclusion in this group, the range of his interests and techniques demonstrates that he is not simply another neorealist. He is the first dramatist consciously to seek a synthesis of the realistic mode with absurdist techniques. What emerges in the Pinter canon is an entirely different approach to drama, one whose roots are widely spread in a variety of recognizable but very different modes and playwrights. Thus, Pinter's work has been met with a wide range of opinion and reaction. Unlike many of his predecessors, he was not reacting against an earlier movement as much as he was trying to reconcile diversity into a unified dramatic vision.

Like Edward Albee, Pinter came to an inherited dramatic tradition that seemed to have nothing new to offer in terms of realism but had also recently witnessed a burst of experimentation in absurdism that was destined to become static, as Beckett's canon demonstrates. But also like Albee, he did not immediately offer a solution to the problem of dramatic diversity, nor has either playwright ceased to experiment with possible means of reconciliation, for both are still quite active, despite the frequency with which their artistic obituaries are published. In the history of contemporary drama, Pinter and Albee are among the first generation of postmoderns, accepting the laurel of Beckett, the last of the moderns. Their well-analyzed plays are highly idiosyncratic and their dramatic aesthetics are intensely personal, thus the wide-spread use of such terms as Albeesque and Pinterese. In literary history, their position is secure, for following them is the "Second Wave" of dramatists, those playwrights whose inheritance is postmodern and who attempt to apply the techniques formulated by Pinter and Albee, playwrights whose inclusion in the Theater of the Absurd has always been forced and artificial.

While Beckett represents one refinement of absurdism, Pinter takes the ground won away from naturalism and refines it further. His chief contribution to dramatic literature is the imposition of Beckettian techniques on realistic conventions. Pinter's world of interiority and archetypal characters is similar to Beckett's, but Pinter strives for immediate identification within a realistic context, attaining an immediate subjectivity rather than the metaphoric level of Beckett. Pinter's characters approach the void of meaninglessness as do Beckett's, but rather than surrendering to despair in a gesture of cosmic symbolism, they attempt to find ways of sustaining themselves in the absence of purpose or meaning. The pessimism of Beckett, which pervades his technique, creating self-contained philosophical statements on stasis, is countered by an inherent optimism in Pinter, whose technique is to suggest possible solutions to meaninglessness, showing in both form and content means of coping with physical reality and daily existence. Both dramatists deal in metaphor, but while Beckett attempts to define man's essence, Pinter concentrates on his existence.

Therefore, while Beckett moves from existentialism into essence, Pinter remains an existentialist, the only playwright today, according to Walter Kerr, who writes existentialist plays existentially. He suggests that Beckett presents only slightly individualized concepts in his works, while "exploratory movement in the void, without preconception or precommittment, should come first. Conceptualization should come later, if at all."[1] Pinter does explore, probing rather than disclosing, attempting to dramatize an existential reality. As Barbara Kreps observes:

> The solitary nature of the mind leaves perception, imagination, and memory free to function on the "facts" of every life in the same way they function on both the creation and apprehension of art. In other words, the uncertain boundaries between where reality ends and art takes over in the creation of life, either in the public theater or in the privacy of one's own rooms, are determined by the existential fact of isolation.[2]

Pinter accepts the existential fact of isolation, attempting to define its limits, rather than simply presenting a statement on the nature of isolation as does Beckett.

Key to an understanding of Pinter's work is a recognition of his inheritance of the interior nature of drama from Beckett. Neither an existentialist nor an absurdist, but a ruthless realist who observes that disorder is internal, not external, Pinter presents an exposition of the interior self in his work. The impulse toward minimalism in his drama and the resulting obscurity of message, clearly inherited from Beckett, is justified by James R. Hollis: "The motive of meaning is formed precisely in man's impulse to overcome through language the apparent barrier between the outer and inner environments which he inhabits."[3]

In Pinter's early works, such as The Room and The Dumb Waiter, this effect is achieved by placing a limited number of characters, often pairs reminiscent of Beckett's, who have no backgrounds presented in exposition, in a room, representing isolation and enclosure and suggestive of regression to the womb, and having them confront an intruder, representative of the unknown or the forces that exist outside the room in society. These "comedies of menace," as they have been categorized, are representations of people confronting the unknown, that which is suppressed within themselves, as in Tea Party, or those forces of society which they have chosen to dismiss, as in The Birthday Party, but whose existence in everyday reality makes it impossible for them to deny.

This paradigm is key to the early Pinter, striving for a universality of situation rather than a universality of condition, as in Beckett. His sets, at least from The Room to The Homecoming, are quite realistic, perhaps even naturalistic in the sense that they insist on the basic and ordinary, and while they quite concretely represent specific locales in each play, they suggest an interchangeable quality; they are the rooms which all people inhabit in ordinary existence. But Pinter's lack of exposition is a technique which he alone has developed; his characters are individual and recognizable, not the allegorical figures of Beckett. He refuses to explicate their backgrounds, both in terms of origin and personality. They simply exist without explanation or justification. Similarly, their motives for action and the motives of the intruders also are unexplained. The reader is presented with a conflict without knowing its origins or motives and, quite often, its outcome. In The Dumb Waiter, for example, Pinter simply presents Ben and Gus by fiat; their origins, occupations, and motives are all ob-

27

scure, and one learns about them through speculation, perhaps, but primarily through analysis of their actions in the play. Pinter is concerned with how his characters react, not with the nature of the action itself or its origins. The existential choice his characters make is the subject of investigation, for these decisions comprise the texture of life, not their motivations, which are unknowable, even by the individual character. Eschewing elementary psychology, Pinter allows the "how" of an action to expose its "why." Martin Esslin observes that "these, to Pinter, are genuine problems: the problems of identity, of motivation, of verification. They are also--so astonishingly is Pinter in tune with the thinking of our epoch--the basic problems of contemporary philosophy and literature."[4] If people are the sum total of their actions, then these actions are the proper realm of study in which to expose what they are. People may be measured for what they are, that is, accumulated choice, rather than what they were, the environmental and hereditary factors within the framework of psychology which were the hallmarks of naturalistic drama and the basis of such significant realistic works as Ibsen's A Doll's House and Ghosts. Claiming that the basic realistic technique of modern character exposition is "cheating," Pinter has commented in interview on the nature of his technique:

> The playwright assumes that we have a great deal of information about all his characters, who explain themselves to the audience. In fact, what they are doing most of the time is conforming to the author's own ideology. They don't create themselves as they go along, they are being fixed on the stage for one purpose, to speak for the author who has a point of view to put over. When the curtain goes up on one of my plays, you are faced with a situation, a particular situation, two people sitting in a room which hasn't happened before, and is just happening at this moment, and we know no more about them than I know about you, sitting at this table. The world is full of surprises. A door can open at any moment and someone will come in. We'd love to know who it is, we'd love to know exactly what he has on his mind and why he comes in, but how often do we know what someone has on his mind or who this somebody and what goes to make him and make him what he is, and what his relationship to others is?

He has also commented on the question of epistemology which underlies his basic dramatic assumptions:

> The desire for verification is understandable but cannot always be satisfied. There are no hard distinctions between what is real and what is unreal, nor between what is true and what is false. The thing is not

28

necessarily either true or false; it can be both true and false. The
assumption that to verify what has happened and what is happening
presents few problems I take to be inaccurate. A character on the stage
who can present no convincing argument or information as to his past
experience, his present behavior or his aspirations, nor give a comprehensive analysis of his motives is as legitimate and as worthy of attention as one who, alarmingly, can do all these things. The more acute the
experience the less articulate its expression.[5]

Thus, reactions to Pinter's plays are intensely subjective, for the characters are presented in a moment of
choice and the reader is forced into identification
with vacillation, as at the ending of The Dumb Waiter.
The action of the drama is at once a particular character in a given situation and an archetypal character
caught in the process of decision, unattached to a
biography which might dictate the nature of that choice
if viewed within standard psychological references; for
example, Ben may or may not choose to kill Gus.

Because of this ambiguity of construction, the
meaning of Pinter's plays becomes equally ambiguous.
Realism in Pinter is a touchstone from which to measure
the depth of one's reaction; he provides a realistic
setting and stage properties and fully individualized
characters, but these sets are also metaphors for the
psyche and his characters are existential everymen,
frozen at the moment of action. Pinter's method is to
apprehend the consciousness, to realize its subsurface
complexities and irrationalities, in a manner similar
to stream-of-consciousness in fiction.

The pattern of interlocking situations on which
Pinter builds his plays is based on a cause and effect
relationship; therefore, they are more closely allied
with the realistic tradition than with the absurd. But
the reality he dramatizes is both subjective and selective, for his characters often respond directly to
personal fear, primal needs, and psychological anxieties, maintaining the realistic framework of the play
while destroying the recognized limits of social
exchange, as in Tea Party when Disson collapses into
his own subjective perceptions. Pinter's primary tool
for achieving this effect is his language. Shifting
from an ordinary conversational mode, externalized
thought often becomes the conversation, underlining
Pinter's presentation of reality as articulation. He
questions the basic epistemological nature of words,
doubting their ability to convey meaning and maintaining the basic distrust of the communicative value of

language evidenced in Beckett. His characters, whose lack of specific background or motivation suggests a view of personality as fluid and in constant movement, are locked into a condition of multiplicity and possibility, and their language attempts to convey this sense of contingency. In a famous passage from The Homecoming, Ruth says:

> Look at me. I . . . move my leg. That's all it is. But I wear . . . underwear . . . which moves with me . . . it . . . captures your attention. Perhaps you misinterpret. The action is simple. It's a leg . . . moving. My lips move. Why don't you restrict . . . your observations to that? Perhaps the fact that they move is more significant . . . than the words which come through them. You must bear that . . . possibility . . . in mind. Silence. [6]

Emphasizing Pinter's belief that reality lies hidden behind language, Ruth points out that actions are more important than words, for people can apprehend what others do while they can only imperfectly understand anything others say. The meanings of both actions and words are obscure and ultimately unknowable, and the individual's best chance for apprehending a subjective reality lies in an ability to perceive actions and to view words as things rather than as surrogate symbols for reality.

While Pinter's plays are largely static, and little action in the conventional sense takes place, the playwright replaces physical action with verbal contact and movement, where words are used as weapons. As in the scene cited above, when she parts from Teddy, calling him "Eddie," saying "Don't become a stranger" (96), Ruth is asserting her control over the other characters. In her verbal battle with Lenny, she establishes her superior mastery of words by undercutting the pun he has just made, and in her good-bye to her husband, she uses a cliché that expands in meaning by its context, revealing the cold impersonality and thus the danger and horror implicit in ordinary configurations of words. Refining the Chekhovian method of an unspoken subtext, Pinter punctuates his speeches of both the educated and the inarticulate with pauses and silences, conveying the importance of what is left unsaid, whether through reluctance or inability. Esslin argues that dramatic dialogue is a form of action and that "Pinter has given us insight into--has, in a certain measure even discovered--the fact that traditional stage dialogue has always greatly overestimated the degree of logic which governs the use of language, the amount of information which language is actually able to impart on the stage—as in life."[7] Pinter's language, therefore, functions on three levels: it accurately represents ordinary colloquial speech; it underscores the range of possible subjective interpretation; and it creates a silent subtext which conveys as much meaning as dialogue by the absence of words. All of these levels, which often function simultaneously, serve to emphasize one of Pinter's main premises, the notion inherited from Beckett that language is an unreliable, if not impossible, means of communication.

The following brief overview of Pinter's aims and techniques may tend to suggest that his canon is static, but he continues to be a relentless experimenter whose dramatic career has many parallels to Beckett's. His first play, The Room (1957), is a comedy of menace which establishes the room as a self-imposed archetypal womb breached by an intruder in the European tradition of fearing invasion by unknown or hostile forces. But once this basic paradigm was established, he has continued to refine his concepts and techniques, and each succeeding play probes more deeply into the nature of contingent, existential reality.

His first full-length play, The Birthday Party (1957), elaborates on his earlier work by creating an existential archetype for the basic human situation, the expulsion from refuge by unknown and unknowable sinister forces. Functioning on many levels, it is in its broadest sense an allegory of the process of mortality, of man in the world. He followed this with The Dumb Waiter (1957), which explores the menace more fully, comparing society to a modern organization that poses a fundamental threat to individuality, if not existence. By the next year, A Slight Ache dramatizes the intruder within the room, locating fear and menace internally and probing the danger of subjective, unfulfilled need. This play was followed by two largely unsuccessful experiments, A Night Out (1959), which is essentially realistic in a traditional sense, and The Dwarfs (1960), which is his only sustained absurdist work.

In the same year, Pinter produced his second full-length work, The Caretaker, which offers the Beckettian polarity of Davies as a tramp, man as an anti-material, homeless quester, and the brothers Aston and Mick as

31

aspects of a single integrated personality; in this, he turns his attention fully toward man's territorial struggles and primal needs. His next important play, The Collection (1961), moves his style into a more realistic phase with more completely individualized and less allegorical characters and his concerns into a full examination of the lack of motivation and the question of verification. Two years later, The Lover appeared as a more probing examination of the fluidity of personality and the undefined, fragmented nature of character. The Homecoming (1965) represents a culmination of the early Pinter and a summation of his previous concerns in its dramatization of psychology as action.

After The Basement (1967), essentially a dream sequence with little basic reality and with striking resemblances to Look Back in Anger, Pinter moved into a new phase of exploration and experimentation. In a manner reminiscent of Krapp's Last Tape, Pinter's interests were turned toward the problems of memory and time. As Kreps notes, "his vision of a world that contains inexplicable forces of aggression that could destroy us at any minute has been replaced by the view that the individual is ultimately incapable of being touched by any world that is not self-defined. Shared time is a myth."[8] Noel King observes a new menace in his work, "temporal rather than spatial, the menace of the past," and notes that although Pinter has yet to produce his version of Breath, his new plays, "shorter, more lyrical--immediately prompted critics to see Pinter's progress as following a Beckettian path towards wordlessness."[9] But Pinter shows no intention of following Beckett's path of self-limitation. While minimalism does characterize his more recent work, it is philosophically and technically an expansion of his early canon, not a reduction. Stephen H. Gale summarizes that "in his career Pinter has written plays that expose the existence of menace, leading to works examining the source of that menace and determining that it is psychologically based, and thence to an exploration of the mind in terms of the interrelated nature of reality, time, and memory."[10]

Landscape (1968) is an interplay of two interior monologues, mixing memory and uncertainty and emphasizing the omnipresence of experience. Silence (1969) presents three such monologues which continue to explore the multi-faceted nature of the past as filtered through memory and the ambiguity and subjectivity of perception. But the culmination of this minimalist experimentation in interiority, and to date the capstone of his dramatic career, is Old Times (1971), his fourth full-length play. Since then, a few plays have appeared which have not made substantial advances in either technique or message. No Man's Land (1975) explores the boundaries of reality and imagination in terms of the opposition between time present and time remembered in what might be viewed as a dramatization of "The Love Song of J. Alfred Prufrock." Betrayal (1978) inverts time and examines from effect to cause in a study of isolation--social, personal, and epistemological. And The Hothouse (1980), written and discarded in 1960, is a comic examination of the inhumanity of man and his institutiions in Pinter's early style.

Old Times is, in its most fundamental way, an elaboration of a remark by Kate: "There are some things one remembers even though they may never have happened. There are things which may never have happened but as I recall them so they take place" (27-28). In a spare setting, three characters are enmeshed in an almost actionless plot in terms of physical activity, wielding words as weapons and shields, and the configuration is essential Pinter: a married couple in a room defend themselves against an intruder. But this battle is no longer territorial, for what is at stake is possession not of things but of concepts, images of self as they range through time, filtered and shaped by memory. Deeley, Anna, and Kate only exist through memory, and the reality of the play is totally subjective (Anna is present and visible in the initial scene yet remains unrecognized until she speaks, asserting her existence through words). By merging the social, subjective, and psychic levels of reality that he had previously explored only in terms of the shift from the internal to the external, Pinter expands the range of his abilities to capture dramatic contingency, to examine man in isolation as he constantly creates and recreates his own identity and existence. Time is a flux in the play, following no chronological continuum, a continuous process of distillation. As in Beckett's study of Proust and in Eliot's Four Quartets, all time is eternally present, and dramatically, the character who can assert personal memory on the others and recreate the past not only dominates, but affirms individual existence by the verbal assertion. Reality has become completely subjective and internalized, and while the situation and the characters are immediately realistic, the action of the play is freed from time and place, even that represented in the play. The reality the readers respond to is the one they immediately perceive, paralleling the situation of the characters.

Reaching back past Beckett to the philosophy of Sartre, Pinter avoids the accusation of nihilism and the production of existential artifact by dramatizing his views rather than letting them shape the drama or lapsing into simple discourse. He chronicles the isolation and anxiety of postmodern existence, probing the means people employ to define themselves and to perceive others. What Pinter offers is not a solution to meaninglessness, but a celebration of possibility. While dramatized choice has a distinct element of menace, it is also basically optimistic, for it celebrates the capacity of the individual mind to choose, to define itself. And the postmodern dramatic emphasis is on the individual mind, both as it is portrayed in the play and as that play is perceived by the reader. Pinter establishes the subjectivity of reality, the fluidity of time and perception, and by remaining nonjudgemental, mirrors the form of his plays in their effect: the reader chooses along with the character, having become enmeshed in the contingency of the dramatic form.

Stylistically, Pinter has expanded the entire concept of language and its function in drama, clearly demonstrating that it is the action. His blending of the realism of Chekhov with the stycomythic lyricism of Beckett allows him to expose levels of meaning beneath but parallel to external realism. His drama of nonaction demonstrates that the essential drama of postmodern humanity is internal and that the dramatist's function is to expose the interior self. As Brecht advocated, Pinter's is an intellectual drama that disturbs, simultaneously alienating his readers by the shifts from objective reality to engaging them in the experience of the subjective, existential reality of the works. His stylization is a decided heightening of reality by betraying the particular to expose the universal. Perhaps his objective stance to his material is his most Brechtian element, however, for his methods demand reader/audience participation. But Pinter's influence continues to be felt in postmodern drama, for he continues to refine the techniques and concepts in each succeeding play, just as does his trans-Atlantic counterpart, Edward Albee.

34

Albee was early heralded in America as the brilliant young playwright and the inheritor and savior of the native dramatic tradition. Like Pinter in Britain, Albee was the first American dramatist to look beyond national boundaries and offer an infusion of Continental experimentalism to a drama that was dominated by the social realism of Miller and the psychological realism of Williams, although neither of these playwrights had produced a major work for some time. And also like Pinter, Albee looked to the European absurdists for his methods, which he turned to an examination of particularly American concerns, recognizing the limits of absurdism but also the value in its expansion of dramatic possibility.

Tom F. Driver observes that "the story of American theater is that of an attempt, not entirely successful, to create an indigenous art for a mass audience that is highly materialistic and is experiencing an astonishingly rapid growth in material power and technical knowledge," adding that the American sensibility has little awareness of man's being born to catastrophe, and that interiority in drama has traditionally been expressed in therapeutic, neo-Freudian terms, seldom, if ever, in terms of Chekhovian tragicomedy.[11] American drama had indeed made significant advances since O'Neill, and in a relatively short period, but one must not fail to note the parallel development with Britain, which had also been fairly static in terms of development since the burst of originality in Shaw. American drama dates from O'Neill, for both America and Britain share the same dramatic heritage before his emergence. Perhaps the lack of a distinctly native tradition in contrast to the British tradition, which stretches back beyond Shakespeare, is the reason why many modern dramatic critics have so frequently deplored the condition of native drama, but by the late 1950s, everyone was willing to herald the emergence of originality. Unlike Pinter, who emerged during the burst of activity of New Wave drama, Albee was alone in his attempts and seemed to be the figure America had been awaiting to revitalize moribund Broadway.

Catapulted into fame and immediately subjected to rigorous scrutiny, Albee has always been simultaneously lauded and reviled, and he continues to suffer from extremes in evaluations of his works. While in the early 1960s, the usually astute Driver could dismiss Albee as "the author of six bad plays,"[12] Tennessee Williams could also say that he "is the only great playwright we've had in America." [13] The inheritor of a realistic Anglo-American tradition, Albee rejected that tradition and looked to Europe, especially to Ionesco and Beckett, and became the first American postmodern dramatist, like Pinter inspiring a new generation of writers whose experimentation has largely escaped the attacks Albee experienced while working in seeming isolation. Rejecting "our one-dimensional dramatic tradition, his search for a new dramatic language is part of a deep-rooted instinct to find adequate expression for the existential dilemma at the heart of the modern experience," asserts Anne Paolucci.[14]

In 1962, while observing that the Theater of the Absurd is either on its way out or undergoing a fundamental change, Albee was able to "submit that The Theatre of the Absurd, in the sense that is is truly the contemporary theater, facing as it does man's condition as it is, is the Realistic theater of our time. . . ."[15] And Paolucci notes that,

The theater of the absurd has struggled to find ways of redefining these essentials, juxtaposing internal landscape and external events, facts and fantasy, reshaping language to suit the splintered action, using everything that the stage offers to do so. But the kind of protagonist that emerges within this new medium is forever threatening to dissolve into a voice, a mind, a consciousness, a strange creature without identity or personality.[16]

Albee, like Pinter, avoids the traps of enclosure and reduction to essence evident in Beckett's work, attempting like the Englishman to achieve a plurality of vision and to avoid creating existential artifacts. Paralleling the course of Pinter's experimentalism, Albee's work continues to explore the means to expand the limits of dramatic reality with each new play, building on the concepts and methods asserted in each succeeding work. Much like Pinter's, his technique is to undercut conventional expectations by dividing his emphasis between external and internal reality. He terms his method "selective reality,"[17] which is a combination of the concept of plastic theater as evidenced in Williams' The Glass Menagerie, a memory play which breaks down the time continuum and portrays a subjective, impressionistic reality, and the metaphorical allusiveness of the Beckett canon. His characters and situations are both specific and general, functioning on one level of reality within the context of the drama as well as suggesting multi-leveled layers of universal significance. His national inheritance is evident in his specific social criticism, an established American convention since the 1920s, and while he criticizes institutions, they are not necessarily specifically American, although they tend to be more specific than the menace, or threat to individuality, evident in Pinter's work.

Often using the family as a microcosm of society, he examines the nature of human bonds in a situation where the present is contingent on both past and future. His realistic framework, the family, serves as the point of departure for his own type of subjective reality, an examination of his characters' psyches, dramatized in as late a play as All Over. Albee's method, as a brief overview of his canon will suggest, is to uncover and reveal the unconscious of his characters, making internal reality his mode and the interplay of personalities and values his dramatic action. His producer, Richard Barr, has noted that "Edward was the first playwright to say that people invent their own illusions to give themselves a reality. And his characters are aware of it. . . . The awareness was what was new."[18]

Albee's subject matter is the conventional system of false values, empty language, and sterile emotion that are the means by which modern individuals, not simply Americans, "illusion" themselves from reality. External reality is not the true reality of modern existence but lies beneath the surface in the individual mind, riddled with its own subjective set of illusions and anxieties. His work is social criticism only insofar as modern individuals are social creatures. He examines people not in the isolation of the room/womb as Pinter does, but in their familial environment, which Albee sees as a cage which separates them from all other people who inhabit their own individual cages. He attacks language as a masking illusion, composed of clichéd conventions which obscure meaning rather than conveying it. In his early plays particularly, such as The American Dream and The Sandbox, where the influence of Ionesco is strongest, the trite speeches of his characters demonstrate their lack of feeling and their inhumanity, the danger and horror of the ordinary, as they avoid communication with those people seemingly closest to them, an effect underscored by their familial situation.

All of Albee's characters experience a glimpse into the void of meaninglessness, but only those who surrender to it become the human wreckage many critics find to be the hallmark of his drama. Even one of the bleakest of his plays, Who's Afraid of Virginia Woolf?, offers the possibility of redemption at the end. If George and Martha, like all his characters, can confront the reality of the emptiness of their lives and throw off their insulating illusion, such as their personal myth of the nonexistent child, then they may have the hope of constructing a subjective validity of existence. Only when stripped of illusion can humanity hope for redemption and salvation, an elevation invariably offered in terms of establishing meaning and assigning value to another person in an honest and aware relationship. While Pinter dramatizes choice on a metaphoric level, examining characters as they construct a method for dealing with life, Albee suggests that self-value is ultimately reflected in one's relationships with others. One must discard lies and evaluate self for what it is, then subjectively construct a set of values that recognize that, while essentially isolated, people give meaning to themselves only by choosing to value other people and by finding strength in others in order to confront the void. While Albee does not deny that the existential reality of life is isolation and a subjective perception of reality, he goes one step further than Pinter by suggesting that people must be social creatures and must establish realistic means for dealing with others. Love and commitment are his chief weapons against meaninglessness.

Like Pinter, Albee's range of experimentation is wide and he continues to produce works that further develop certain basic premises. His first play, The Zoo Story (1959), examines the isolation of modern life and argues for the need and difficulty of meaningful, as opposed to empty, human communication. Humans are no better than animals if they refuse to recognize the presence of their cage and then break out of it and touch another human being. Realistically grounded, the play uses standard absurdist techniques to heighten reality and to suggest its internal quality, for while it hinges dramatically on the murder/suicide of Jerry, the resolution is in Peter's psyche, as he, like the reader, struggles to make sense of what he has experienced. The Death of Bessie Smith (1960) is more clearly rooted in external reality and explores the social cages created by gender, race, profession, and psychology, pointing out the disparity between things as they are and things as they should be.

Following this venture into psychological realism, he produced The Sandbox (1960) and The American Dream (1961), two absurdist plays that are variations on a theme and are paradigmatic of the early Albee. Evidencing the strong influence of both Ionesco and Beckett, these episodic works are constructed of linking situations and employ conventional, cliché-ridden language. While the three generations of family members function allegorically to point out the emptiness of modern life as well as to direct several important social attacks, their primary function is to underscore the isolation and lack of communication in relationships externally structured on love but internally founded on lies and sterility. Time past (Grandma) is discarded by the mechanized and inhuman present (the solipsistic Mommy and emasculated Daddy), whose heir is the empty and materialistic young man (the American Dream), the personification of anesthetized external beauty who will do anything for money. He is the future of the modern individual who refuses to place value on internal qualities.

These allegorized metaphors of modern humanity give way to the more realistic and specific characters of his first full-length play, Who's Afraid of Virginia Woolf? (1962). A dramatization of the empty ritual by which people insulate themselves from an awareness of themselves, the play exposes the internal horror beneath the surface of ordinary social interaction as the characters flail about in the void of meaninglessness without attempting to face the reality of their lives and construct a sense of subjective worth and direction. Enclosed in their room, George and Martha savage each other in an attempt to externalize the blame for the emptiness of their lives, which are based on multiple illusions, such as the imaginary child and George's ascension to the presidency of the college. Only at the end of the play when they have brutally stripped each other of these illusions does the possibility exist of facing reality. At the close of Act III, "The Exorcism," Martha admits her fear of Virginia Woolf, the fear of madness in denying reality, as she and George retire to rest for the new day, literally and metaphorically the new beginning of their lives together. While quite specifically about two people in a specific situation, wielding words as weapons to cloak reality, the play is also open to metaphoric interpretations reminiscent of Beckett's work. The roots of American idealism are suggested by their names, the disparity between public existence (Nick and

Honey) and private reality (George and Martha) is
contrasted, and one can read the play as a conflict
between failed history (George) and the new methods of
science (Nick). Thus, this play, as is characteristic
of all of Albee's plays, functions in a specific way,
exploring the layers of subjective reality, as well as
in a general way, providing metaphors for many of the
conflicts of modern existence.

Albee's next effort was at sustained religious
allegory, Tiny Alice (1964), and is a not altogether
successful attempt at presenting subjective, existential reality in symbolic terms. His restrained A
Delicate Balance (1966) is perhaps Albee's finest
exploration of existential terror in its attempts to
probe his basic philosophic preoccupations within a
realistic framework. Like Beckett and Pinter, he takes
this idea to further dramatic extremes in his brace of
experimental works, Box and Quotations from Chairman
Mao Tse-tung (1968). These theatrical attempts at
allegorical minimalism are lyrical intertwinings of
interior monologues which attempt to present objective
and subjective reality simultaneously.

However, Albee returned to his more characteristic
realistic mode with his next works, All Over (1971) and
Seascape (1975), which were originally planned as
companion pieces under the collective title of Life and
Death. The former is a modern morality play, at once
naturalistic and symbolic, which eschews exposition and
explores the veiling nature of memory and the subjectivity of time. Clearly Pinteresque in technique, it
remains characteristic of Albee in its final insistence
on human values and the abandonment of illusion for
personal salvation. The latter play defies external
reality by presenting two lizards as human prototypes
in its attempt to dramatize a collapse of time, confronting modern humanity with what it once was. By
suggesting that individuals must assume a stance of
negative capability and confront the unknowns of life
boldly, Albee once again affirms the power of emotion
in the renewed, realistic bond between Charlie and
Nancy, his existential everymen.

The following year, Albee again returned to
Beckettian (and Pinteresque) experimentation with
Listening, an exploration of the subjectivity of
perception. His allegorized--yet specific--Man and
Woman are portraits in isolation and the inability to
communicate as they drift in the haze of memory, de-

tached from time, exploring the impossibility of verification of self. Counting the Ways (1977) continues
this exploration into minimalism and subjectivity, as
He and She maintain their own delicate balance,
threatened with non-existence. Affirming love at the
conclusion, it charts the impossibility of knowing or
communicating anything, especially redemptive emotion.
Reality for these characters is completely subjective
as they attempt to break through their cages of isolation; they realize the impossibility of empirical
knowledge yet the necessity of affirmation as She
responds to his "Do you love me?" with "I think I
do."[19]   Albee's recent play, The Lady from Dubuque
(1979), is a return to the realistic mode. It presents
a social group of characters who are nonetheless isolated from each other despite the elaborate network of
connections they have imposed on their lives. Person-
ified psychological states, they represent individual
reactions to nothingness. Again, he underscores the
subjectivity of reality by insisting that no matter
what social bonds we construct to illusion ourselves,
we are essentially alone. Contemporary people can find
sustenance in love and the courage to face the unknown,
but their reactions and values are intensely personal.

John von Szeliski states that "in Edward Albee's A
Delicate Balance we have the most significant representation of the essence, and the effective treatment, of
a world view of the 1960s or the 1970s."[20]   Awarded a
Pulitzer Prize (which many people maintain was a conso-
lation for losing it with Who's Afraid), this play is
perhaps the best example of the polarity in Albee
criticism, but many of the attacks on the play may be
surprise reactions to the uncharacteristic understate-
ment of the work. It is an examination of free-float-
ing anxiety, the "Terror," to which all human beings
are susceptible, manifested here as a failure of love
and a fear of isolation. The balance of the title is
the delicate line which separates reality from illusion, which the typical Albee couple, Agnes and Tobias,
try to walk. In Pinteresque fashion, they inhabit
their room, insulated from reality, and face threats
from all sides; they are poised between extremes in
their own family, for Claire represents escape in
self-withdrawal and Julia is escape in flight. Faced
with varieties of isolation, from cynicism to romance
within their own family structure, they have to confront the Terror brought into their home by intruders,
their best friends, Edna and Harry.

The power of the drama arises from its shift from the external to the internal, from objective to subjective reality, and the conclusion is much like that of Who's Afraid: battle weary, scarred, and exhausted, Agnes and Tobias, like George and Martha, have undergone an ordeal and are indeed drained, but they lack the cushioning illusion they held at the beginning of the play which separated them from self-awareness and from each other. Agnes' closing line, "Come now; we can begin the day" (170), holds the promise of a new beginning, a brutal facing of reality highly reminiscent of the sunrise in Ibsen's Ghosts. While apparently less than they once were, the characters have achieved a new potentiality simply by losing what they once had: the illusions that made them withdraw into the room in isolation from each other and the world. Having glimpsed the void, their fear is generalized as a fear of meaninglessness or nothingness, but it has specific applications as well. Their lives are obviously not what they had been trying to believe they were, for the concept of family and the ritual of communication are empty, merely gestures to maintain the illusion of emotion and meaning where none actually exist. So not only do they fear an abstract philosophical concept, they fear the emptiness and isolation of their collective and individual lives as well.

As in Pinter's work, the menace in this play is an abstraction, but Albee goes further by giving it very specific applications as well. While the nature of action in Pinter is relatively unimportant, since he stresses the importance of the decision process itself, Albee maintains that action is vital while suggesting the nature of the action: people must strip themselves of illusion, bond themselves to one another, and emerge from their rooms to face the daylight of shared reality. Subjective reality is every individual's terrain and the realm of personal consciousness, but it is isolating. Fragmented subjective realities must be bound together to form a collective, for people cannot retreat from the society of which they are a part, even if the unit is as small as a marriage or a family. Like Pinter, studying the response to external demands, Albee presents the fear by fiat; nothingness is an existential reality. His concern is with how his characters deal with abstractions, with the choices they make. Action in the face of contingency is the primary postmodern dramatic subject.

As in Beckett and Pinter, Albee's plays generally

begin in recognizable, external reality and shift to specific explorations of inner realities within the characters. His method of selective reality within a traditional framework allows him to expand the limits of conventional realism by dramatizing characters in the process of self-exploration, stripping away the layers of illusion to reach the emptiness of their lives, the naked masks of Pirandello. But Albee is not content with a dramatization of choice and his characters are not stalemated abstractions, such as Reader in Ohio Impromptu or even Disson in Tea Party. They are recognizable, individualized characters who reach their lower depths and stand stripped of false notions of self, attaining a universality by their nakedness. Albee's drama is a celebration of the possibility of ascent, of the possibility of redefining self and emerging from isolation to make contact with others. His optimism lies in his belief in redemptive emotion, a positive valuation of one's self and one's fellow human beings. Albee may be cynical about the difficulty involved in the struggle for self-awareness, but his drama concludes with possibility. The thunder in the drama holds a tentative promise of rain in the existential wasteland of postmodern existence.

In summary, both Pinter and Albee represent a distinct break with the Beckettian tradition, itself a fusion of realism and experimentalism. Their plays stand at the crossroads of twentieth-century drama, and various attempts have been made to place them technically and historically, the most important theories being dissonance, compressionism, and contextualism. While each of these views has its merits, both playwrights must be viewed as unique transition figures, the first of the postmoderns, for whom no specific categories are immediately applicable.

In the Beckettian tradition of minimalism and the movement toward essence, some plays by Pinter and Albee, such as Landscape and Box, have been viewed by Robert Mayberry as comprising a theater of dissonance or discord, "the disassociation of the visual and the verbal media"; similar in form to the interplay between objective and subjective reality which characterizes all these plays, this particular theory asserts that "Beckett relocated the central conflict traditionally found in a struggle between characters to the more abstract level of conflicting media," placing the dramatic actions of the plays within the minds of the readers.[21] Both Pinter and Albee have returned to con-

43

ventional forms that adhere to a basic realistic tradition after their experiments in theatricality, yet they
preserve the effect of dissonance. Within a recognizable mode of external reality, their plays probe the
consciousnesses of individual characters, exposing at
once the social framework of their lives as well as
their interiority. The juxtaposition of the specific
and the general, the subjective and the objective, the
particular and the universal, the interior and the
exterior, the imagistic and the metaphoric, creates
both the plurality of form and response, defying probability for possibility to engage readers to the limits
of their own awareness. These dramas expand from the
specificity of the text to the consciousness of the
characters to the perception of the reader. Meaning in
these plays spirals inward to the point where it is
given substance only in response to the dramatic
action. Readers are at once alienated from a form
which seems familiar on the surface but thwarts their
expectations while they are actively engaged in the
resolution of the action and the assignment of value.
The subjectivity of reality, therefore, embraces read-
er/audience perception, and the postmodern form is one
which simultaneously alienates and engages.

Noting that absurdism denies the "weapons" of
traditional drama, Laurence Kitchin observes that the
mode "attacks us below the threshold of consciousness,
mainly by visual devices and by language in a state of
fragmentation, in short, by a kind of intellectual
clowning." Dismissing absurdism as a fruitless experiment in form, Kitchin goes on to maintain that the two
basic forms of postmodern drama are the epic and compressionism, the latter being plays "in which the
characters are insulated from society in such a way as
to encourage the maximum conflict of attitudes." [22]
While such a term aptly describes the works of Pinter
and Albee, it tends to suggest the theatricalism of the
late Beckett canon more than the existential realism of
the postmoderns. Maintaining that realism, not theatricalism, is the essential mode of modern drama, John
Gassner argues for a contextual view of drama that
results in the "coexistence of realism and non-realis-
tic stylization turned into an active and secure part-
nership in the interests of essential realism." He
observes that,

In one way or another, modern drama has again and again manifested an
Instinct for organization, as against disorganization; a feeling for
crescendo, as against decrescendo, stasis, and circularity; a regard for

language, as against a disregard for it in favor of silent mimesis or mime; and, in general, a marked esthetic orientation, as against a sense of disintegration and chaos.[23]

The tension between these impulses is precisely the difference in direction between Beckett and his successors, Pinter and Albee. They reject his dissolution into essence and insist on a dramatic portrayal of existence, and their works are contextual in a similar sense to which the term was originally applied to poetry, relying on tensions of context rather than direction, probing and displaying vertical depth rather than horizontal movement.

As Marvin Rosenberg observes, the modern impulse is to hold time at bay, to circumscribe the present and to isolate a non-narrative felt life. He points out that this impulse can follow two paths, toward the "pure," a theatrical embodiment of a mental state, where the character becomes a transparent image rather than an intermediate symbol (as in Godot), or becomes a condition of living (as in the late Beckett); or it can follow traditional development, wherein character is extended in dimension (as in Death of a Salesman). As Rosenberg maintains, contextual drama seeks to represent the psyche which rebels against pattern,[24] but as Bert O. States points out, Rosenberg's concept of contextual form is actually a description of effect. He maintains that the plays of the "New drama" "do not imitate actions, they imitate the mind; or, in clearer terms, these plays do not have plots, they have psychology."[25] The positions of both scholars are extremes, for postmodern drama, as established by Pinter and Albee, seeks to dramatize consciousness detached from time, and the action or plot is the interplay of individually apprehended consciousnesses and subjective evaluations of reality. Reality is what the individual character (and reader) apprehends it to be, and the dramatic action is often the disparity between one view and another or between perceived and external reality. What appears to be a realistic drama staged in terms of external reality is found to be actually unfolding on the level of the subconscious, and it is on this level that it has its effect on the reader. The external framework acts as a touchstone to measure the depth of the playwright's probing into subjective perception. By the continual interplay between external and internal reality, readers are able to chart the depth and progress of their own involvement in the play. The readers' positions and responsi-

45

bilities are to integrate the two (or more) levels of reality and draw their own subjective conclusions. Thus, in the most Brechtian manner are the readers involved in the work, and they must apprehend the totality of the dramatic experience to interpret it, for the form is decidedly not discursive in the traditional sense. Even the language is unreliable, for text often serves only to point to a more important subtext, which underscores the essential literary condition of postmodern drama, for form and content are inseparable, and while performance adds another dimension to the individual play, direct interpretation of the text alone discloses the theatrical and dramatic intentions of the playwright.

Pinter and Albee effectively point the direction for the unification of the late modern interior view of the human condition with traditional realism in an effective, integrated form. Their adaptation of experimental techniques, especially those advocated by Beckett and the other absurdists, to conventional form has allowed an expansion of possibility for the exploration of a paradoxically reduced postmodern concern, the existential reality of human existence. The individual applications of these concepts by a new generation of dramatists signal the establishment of a distinctly postmodern dramatic literary aesthetic.

Notes

[1] Harold Pinter (New York: Columbia Univ. Press, 1967), pp. 3, 6.

[2] "Time and Harold Pinter's Possible Realities: Art as Life, and Vice Versa," Modern Drama, 22 (1979), 59.

[3] Harold Pinter: The Poetics of Silence (Carbondale: Southern Illinois Univ. Press, 1970), p. 1.

[4] Pinter: A Study of His Plays, expanded ed. (New York: Norton, 1976), p. 38.

[5] Quoted in Esslin, pp. 38-39, 40.

[6] Harold Pinter, The Homecoming, in Complete Works: Three (New York: Grove, 1978), pp. 68-69; subsequent references to the various plays in this four volume edition will appear as page numbers in parentheses in the text.

[7] Esslin, p. 211.

[8] Kreps, p. 56.

[9] "Pinter's Progress," Modern Drama, 23 (1980), 250, 247.

[10] "The Variable Nature of Reality: Harold Pinter's Plays in the 1970s," Kansas Quarterly, 12 (1980), 17.

[11] Romantic Quest and Modern Query (New York: Delacorte, 1970), pp. 285, 321-22.

[12] "What's the Matter with Edward Albee?" in The Modern American Theater, ed. Alvin B. Kernan (Englewood Cliffs, NJ: Prentice-Hall, 1967), p. 99.

[13] Quoted in Richard E. Amacher, Edward Albee (New York: Twayne, 1969), p. 170.

[14] From Tension to Tonic: The Plays of Edward Albee (Carbondale: Southern Illinois Univ. Press, 1972), pp. 10, 5.

[15] Quoted in John Gassner, Directions in Modern Theatre and Drama (New York: Holt, Rinehart and Winston, 1966), p. 334.

[16] Paolucci, p. 10.

[17] Quoted in Amacher, p. 34.

[18] Quoted in David Richards, "Edward Albee: Who's Afraid of the Critics?" Clarion-Ledger [Jackson, MS], 18 Feb. 1982, Sec. C, p. 8.

[19] Edward Albee, Counting the Ways, in The Plays (New York: Atheneum, 1982), III, 51; subsequent references to the various plays in this four volume edition will appear as page numbers in parentheses in the text.

[20] Tragedy and Fear (Chapel Hill: Univ. of North Carolina Press, 1971), p. 23.

[21] "A Theatre of Discord: Some Plays of Beckett, Albee, and Pinter," Kansas Quarterly, 12 (1980), 7.

[22] Drama in the Sixties (London: Faber and Faber, 1966), pp. 30, 21, 46; see also his "Compressionism: The Drama of the Trapped," New Hungarian Quarterly, 18 (1965), 188-90.

[23] Gassner, pp. 354, 358; italics in the original.

[24] "A Metaphor for Dramatic Form," in Gassner, pp. 342-50.

[25] "The Case for Plot in Modern Drama," Hudson Review, 20 (Spring 1967), 52-53.

FOUR: TOM STOPPARD
Intellectual Gymnast

Perhaps foremost among the young playwrights who comprise the first recognizable generation of post-modern dramatists is Tom Stoppard. Although Victor L. Cahn sees Stoppard as the first of the post-absurd-ists,[1] the playwright is clearly working in a direct line of descent from Pinter and Albee as they have developed the advances made by Beckett. Stoppard has noted that <u>Waiting for Godot</u> "redefined the minima of theatrical validity," and that "Prufrock and Beckett are the two syringes of my diet, my arterial system."[2] Stoppard's admiration of Eliot is evident throughout his work (in such references as his description of Switzerland as "the still centre of the wheel of war" in <u>Travesties</u>), and many of the poet's concerns, such as the nature of time and the search for a viable metaphysic in a postmodern world, are the playwright's also. The other master of modernism, James Joyce, has a recognizable effect on Stoppard's work as well; his dramatic technique borrows much from the author of <u>Ulysses</u>, and Joyce appears as a character in <u>Travesties</u>. His attention to effects and devices in the other genres adds to the self-conscious literary effect that his plays possess, and he is seen by some critics as an intellectual popularizer and light-weight. But Stoppard's work is a drama of ideas, and more like Sartre than his immediate predecessors, Stoppard often writes plays which directly deal with philosophical ideas, such as <u>Jumpers</u>, as well as making his works inherently philosophical in structure, such as <u>Rosencrantz and Guildenstern Are Dead</u>. Rather than being a superficial attempt at creating a new drama of philosophy like Sartre's, however, Stoppard's plays reflect the postmodern obsession with ideas, which form the basis of his work and are most often his subject matter. His canon is no less a philosophical statement than that of any modern playwright, for unlike Sartre, he is primarily a dramatist and not a philosopher. His vision is a reflection of postmodern concerns, and, as

Clive James notes, "the appropriate analogies to Stoppard's vision lie just as much in modern physics as in modern philosophy." [3]

Whether Stoppard's philosophical vision is expressly existential has been a subject of debate. Maintaining that he personally believes that "anybody's set of ideas which grows out of the play [in this case, Rosencrantz and Guildenstern Are Dead] has its own validity," he has said that he "didn't know what the word 'existential' meant until it was applied to Rosencrantz. And even now existentialism is not a philosophy I find either attractive or plausible." [4] Agreeing with Stoppard, Sir Alfred Ayer, whose philosophical beliefs form a large part of Jumpers, remarked that "existentialism works much better in the theatre than in theory." [5] Kenneth Tynan sees Stoppard's beliefs as arising from three basic premises: "the intrinsic merits of individualism," "a universe in which everything is relative, yet in which moral absolutes exist," and "the probability that this paradox can be resolved only if we accept the postulate of a presiding deity." [6] While this may be true in terms of the playwright's personal vision, an explicitly Christian stance is not what appears in the plays, for no one system embraces all reality. Stoppard himself has noted that "there is very often no single, clear statement in my plays" (6), and his work reflects postmodern existence by its celebration of multiplicity, by its presentation of alternatives. While an explicitly Christian reading of his work would be a mistake, an existential reading would be equally myopic. Stoppard maintains that his work "can be interpreted in existential terms, as well as in other terms" (6). Like Pinter and Albee, Stoppard refuses to judge, preferring to make his readers his accomplices by forcing them into judgement for themselves.

While Stoppard's beliefs are probably more closely aligned with those of the author of Principia Ethica, or more specifically, with those of his own George Moore in Jumpers, where philosophical debate is most clearly displayed, his arguments are essentially humanistic and eschew the specific for the universal. He avoids asserting a single basis for interpretation by examining the common roots of many lines of philosophical inquiry. Like Pinter, Stoppard attempts to explore these questions rather than to provide simple answers to them. He is concerned with the nature of the choices people make, not the specific actions themselves, and if any particular concern can be singled out as his primary concern, the issue of morality is central to all of his philosophical speculation. Noting that the objective of art is universal perception, he has stated that "art--Auden or Fugard or the entire caldron--is important because it provides the moral matrix, the moral sensibility from which we make our judgements about the world" (14). While irreducible to either Christian or existential foundations, Stoppard's vision is moral, and his concern is with the nature of human choice, and although his beliefs are conservative, they are not necessarily pessimistic. His characters are often dramatized in failure, and while there may be evidence of sympathetic identification on the playwright's part, the failure is confined to a specific choice and does not necessarily imply the failure of modern philosophy.

The lack of clarity in the statements presented in the plays reflects Stoppard's dramatic technique. He has said: "I tend to write through a series of small, large and microscopic ambushes--which might consist of a body falling out of a cupboard, or simply an unexpected word in a sentence." His stated goal is "to end up by contriving the perfect marriage between the play of ideas and farce or perhaps even high comedy" (6-7), and his work is a comedic and farcical presentation of serious thought. As in Pinter's comedies of menace, the humor only extends to a certain point in the plays, after which it serves to underscore the essential seriousness of what is occurring. Rejecting the established forms of comedy and tragedy, Stoppard's blending of the two represents a realistically blended vision of life, one which attempts to reproduce the actual texture of existence without excluding any of its components. He rejects the standard tools of modern dramatists, including abstract expressionism and naturalism, which he feels leads to "the dregs of bad theatre."[7] His technique is to pick and choose from traditional devices to create a blending of styles which is particularly his own, such as the mélange in Travesties, discarding whatever seems to limit the presentation of subjective reality. The juxtaposition of styles in his work reflects the multiplicity of contemporary views of existence. His comedy arises largely from logically extending his action one step further than it exists in objective reality.

While his works have close affinities with the Theater of the Absurd, Stoppard's work does not attempt to make statements about the absurdity of existence by breaking causality in his plays. To the contrary, his comments on absurdity and the chaos of his plots arise from his insistence on logic and reason. He returns to the traditional dramatic structure of cause and effect, and through the relentless application of logic, he dramatizes it as inherently absurd. The effect is similar to the effect of explicitly absurd drama but is manifested more as farce, a precursor to absurdity. Therefore, he appropriates the spirit of absurdity rather than the technique, arriving at many of the same conclusions without achieving the identical effect, as he does in Rosencrantz, Jumpers, and Travesties.

The chaos of his plays is the disorder of reason, the multiplicity of possible action rather than the stasis of nonaction. Episodic rather than linear, his plots are similar to Pinter's in construction and Beckett's in effect; his events adhere to cause and effect relationships which govern external reality while betraying the particular to convey the universal in presenting subjective reality. This almost symbolic action can take many forms, such as wish-fulfillment, as in Cecily's strip-tease in Travesties, or actualized metaphor, as in the symbolic presence of the screen in Jumpers. Felicia Hardison Londré argues that "dialectical thought provides some impetus for advancing the action in Jumpers, but it is the externalization of that thought in theatrical images that makes this play the supreme dramatic achievement in Stoppard's canon to date," and that "Travesties repeats the pattern, and falls only a little short of that mark as a piece of writing, although it may have an edge over Jumpers in the theater."[8] Like Pinter and Albee, Stoppard relies on externalized thought as a means for presenting a subjective reality and employs a variety of theatrical devices to exploit his intention, including the very Brechtian devices of song and documentary. In his work, reality is "thin," "the name we give to the common experience";[9] in any play, it is the collection of individually perceived notions of reality of each of the characters, who inevitably function on different planes of reality simultaneously. Thus, Rosencrantz combines both the play of the two courtiers in a modern idiom and Shakespeare's Hamlet in its structure, and Travesties juxtaposes dadaist, aesthetic, and political realities while presenting multiple versions of certain scenes. Stoppard attempts to expose subjective reality within the framework of traditional objective and external reality, as do his predecessors, but rather than dramatizing subtle shifts between the two levels, he presents many different levels in seeming chaos simultaneously.

While Stoppard's plays juxtapose different levels of reality, they are also embodiments of different realities in their forms. Exploiting various resources of the theater, the works emphasize their own theatricality by being grounded in other dramatic works. He has called his first work, Walk on Water, revised as Enter a Free Man, "Flowering Death of a Salesman," and another early play, The Gamblers, produced once in 1965, "Waiting for Death in the Condemned Cell" (4), acknowledging the direct influences of Bolt, Miller, and Beckett. But what may appear as youthful admiration in the early Stoppard is actually the beginning of an important dramatic method, the appropriation and exploration of implications in existing dramas. One of the subjects of travesty in Travesties is Oscar Wilde's The Importance of Being Earnest, and Rosencrantz is a version of the off-stage action of characters who are on stage in Hamlet. His drama is decidedly intellectual, but not inaccessible, as a charge of elitism might imply, for while Stoppard is undeniably aware that intellectual speculation in itself may be an empty exercise, the tools of philosophy do indeed bear upon ordinary existence. Responding to the intellectual bases of the motives of Epic Theater, Stoppard celebrates the ordinary in his borrowings from other plays. Rosencrantz and Guildenstern are peripheral to Shakespeare's work, and Stoppard's play is a careful examination of their very ordinary existence. And while Travesties concerns major artists, artistic movements, and revolution, its basis is in the memory of Henry Carr, a very ordinary and undistinguished man whose only previous claim to immortality lies in his existence as a minor character in Ulysses. Stoppard's technique is to explore the everyday and the common against a backdrop of the important and significant: the courtiers against Hamlet, George Moore's personal crisis of faith against the ascendency of the Radical Liberals, Carr's petty grouse against World War I, the rise of modernism, and the Russian Revolution. And often his method is to employ a vehicle most immediately accessible to an enlightened and aware theatrical audience, a dramatic classic. While his plays can be enjoyed as theatrical amusements, their value does not lie in their ability to divert, but rather in their insistence on subjective thought. His "borrowings" simply provide a point of reference for his readers and constitute one of his "ambushes," for his concerns are not with the greatness of the plays on which he bases his, but the very commonness they exclude.

Stoppard has remarked that "what I like to do is take a stereotype and betray it, rather than create an original character. I never try to invent characters. All my best characters are clichés."[10] The exposition of the ordinary within a significant and recognizable context is characteristic of the playwright, and while his technique does result in recognizable individuals, three-dimensional characters, his works are not so much character studies as they are dramatizations of the interplay and conflict of opposing stances. In its most obvious manifestation, the appearances of Lenin, Joyce, and Tzara in Travesties are not significant as creating characters out of the historical figures, but are important as dramatizing them as embodiments of the philosophies they represent. For example, while Joyce is given life as a character in the play, one which has proven acceptable and enlightening even for Joycians, he figures in the work's meaning as a father of modernism, as the intellectual impetus behind Ulysses. Stoppard observes that "my characters are all mouthpieces for points of view rather than explorations of individual psychology. They aren't realistic in any sense. I write plays of ideas uneasily married to comedy or farce."[11] While the plays may be seen as dramatized philosophical conflict, they are always intensely objective in their presentation.

In Pinter and Albee, one can observe the obvious attempt to chart subjective reality as the individual mind perceives it; Stoppard's method is the same, but carried one step further. His concern with subjective perception transcends the individual character and attempts to present the significance of that method of perception. His concern is not so much with characters as individuals, but as points of view. The result is not a conflict of individuals, but a conflict of ideologies. While his interest transcends the individual characters, it does not exclude them. If, as demonstrated in both Pinter and Albee, personality is multiple in subjective response to reality, the individual responses are not as significant as the bases from which they spring. His plays, therefore, demonstrate how individuals respond to contingent reality as a result of their explorations into why that response is both subjective and multiple.

Similar to Stoppard's interest in the multiplicity of human personality is his concern with consciousness and perception. Common to his technique in all his plays is what Virginia E. Leonard terms "a clash of realities," wherein "reality is defined according to personal perception."[12] Necessarily, if each character functions dramatically according to an individual level of perception, the form of the play will be fragmentary and diversified. The farcical nature of his work is rooted largely in this multiplicity and much of the dramatic conflict arises from the inherent differences in these perceptions. All of his characters are basically isolated, within their own concerns and in the way they perceive them, thus making reality a highly individualized process of perception. The essential loneliness of these individuals is dramatized in terms of subjective consciousness, for the reality they perceive is actualized on stage, resulting in a juxtaposition of seemingly bizarre stage properties and dramatic styles. This juxtaposition is evident in the superimposition of Shakespeare's Hamlet upon the post-modern confusion of Stoppard's courtiers; the disparity between the bedroom with its luxurious and the techno-logical conveniences with the academic asceticism of the study, representing the quite different perceptions of reality held by Dotty and George in Jumpers; and the diversity of styles in Travesties, itself imposed upon Wilde's play: lecture, burlesque, limerick, parody of Ulysses, and the repetition of scenes in different styles. Significantly, there is no resolution of these oppostions in the plays, and the protagonists suffer from the same confusion that is reflected in the plots. There is no objective reality in Stoppard's plays, unlike those of Pinter and Albee, which use external reality as a touchstone. Stoppard's characters are awash in their own freedom of choice, and no truth is knowable or absolute, for individual consciousness defines the subjective nature of the reality it per-ceives.

While seldom lyrical, as in Beckett, or realisti-cally subtextual, as in Pinter, Stoppard's language is designed to convey both emotion and meaning, much like Albee's use. But while extremely articulate and self-consciously intellectual, his language is based on verbal turns which obscure and layer meaning verti-cally. The wit, and much of the comedy, of his lan-guage relies on the pun (both verbal and visual), allusion, parody, and abuses of logic, all of which have distinct meanings on the surface, but immediately multiply. Rather than conveying meaning, his language creates a multiplicity of meanings, no one of which is ultimately more definite than any other. In Jumpers, which pits George's Christian morality against logical positivism, this problem is most fully explored, and as embodied in the opposition between Moore and Jumper, this problem is voiced often in this play as it is throughout the canon. For example:

> ARCHIE: Crouch says he saw what, George?
> GEORGE: Well, he didn't actually see . . .
> ARCHIE: Quite. We just don't know.
> GEORGE: There are many things I know which are not verifiable but nobody can tell me I don't know them, and I think that I know that something happened to poor Dotty and she somehow killed McFee, as sure as she killed my poor Thumper.[13]

Ironically, and naturally within the context of the work, George is wrong, for George himself inadvertently kills the hare, although the murder, around which the play is structured, is never solved; nothing is verifiable and no truth is knowable, and intuition is just as fallible as empiricism within the context of subjective reality.

By externalizing thought and probing the subconscious to reveal the interiority of the individual's essential reality, Stoppard's plays are also concerned with memory, especially Travesties, which has its basis in the protagonist's memory. To attempt any form of self-definition demands an assessment of the past, and Stoppard's characters are as paralyzed by the multiplicity of the past as they are by the present; like present reality, past reality, particularly as filtered through memory, is unverifiable, contingent, and subjective. Guildenstern muses: "We cross our bridges when we come to them and burn them behind us, with nothing to show for our progress except a memory of the smell of smoke, and a presumption that once our eyes watered" (61). In Stoppard, the past is as diverse as the present, and any attempt to exercise memory is as doomed to fail as the use of logic or faith.

Rejecting the minimalism and movement toward essence which result in emotional response rather than the intellectual reaction that characterizes Beckett's dramatic progress, Stoppard, like Pinter and Albee, retains many of the basic absurdist devices and aims. He insists on the interior nature of reality and the subjectivity of perception which emphasize the primacy

56

of the individual consciousness. He also evidences a
basic distrust of discourse and the communicative power
of language and creates his drama imagistically on both
specific and general levels. Similarly to Pinter, he
remains objective and explores reactions and the nature
of choice, dramatizing points of view intellectually as
a celebration of possibility; like Albee's, his work is
an interplay of personalities and values without,
however, insisting that his characters strip themselves
of illusion. As in his predecessors, his action is
verbal and time is broken, and his drama is characterized by the individual mind defining itself. Having
adopted the basic postmodern concerns and techniques,
Stoppard's vision is nonetheless highly individual.

Stoppard's critical success was immediate after the
production of what he identifies as his twelfth play,
Rosencrantz and Guildenstern Are Dead (1966). One of
the play's central contributions to dramaturgy is the
distinction made among postmodern views of absurdity.
The coin tossing episode which opens the play and
serves as a major motif demonstrates the helplessness
of ordinary people in controlling their own destiny and
the breakdown of cause and effect relationships as
motivating a moral system of reward and punishment.
All action is shown to be contingent. The Player
outlines his function: "We follow directions--there is
no choice involved. The bad end unhappily, the good
unluckily" (80). To a degree, this illustrates the
central premise of the Theater of the Absurd and suggests a distinctly existential stance, but this is only
one dimension in a complex work. The predicament of
ordinary people enmeshed in a system that they find
incomprehensible, reminiscent of The Dumb Waiter,
suggests the relativity of the meaning of any action,
and this particular situation, the coin tossing, also
serves to suggest a technique characteristic of Stoppard: the extension of logic beyond its logical boundaries. Therefore, the tossing motif reflects Stoppard's dramatization of multiple possibilities on its
surface level, for there are two sides to every coin,
represented by this verbal and visual pun. It also
supports an existential interpretation by suggesting
the breakdown of probability and the meaninglessness of
action, thus demonstrating reason taken to an extreme.
As Guildenstern considers, the appearance of heads
ninety-two times could be the result of a metaphysical
cause and effect situation or divine intervention, but
just as easily, it could be "a spectacular vindication
of the principle that each individual coin spun indi-

vidually . . . is as likely to come down heads as tails and therefore should cause no surprise each individual time it does" (16).

The coin tossing is paradigmatic of the entire play, which examines the individual's capacity to control life and to understand the events of life intellectually by means of empirical reasoning. Guildenstern, like Estragon the more intellectual of the pair, fears the unknown, the incomprehensibility of life that is represented by death, and attempts to assess his position:

> Wheels have been set in motion, and they have their own pace, to which we are . . . condemned. Each move is dictated by the previous one--that is the meaning of order. If we start being arbitrary it'll just be a shambles: at least, let us hope so. Because if we happened, just happened to discover, or even suspect, that our spontaneity was part of their order, we'd know that we were lost. (60)

Followed by the story of the Chinese philosopher who destroyed the distinction between objective and subjective reality for himself by dreaming that he was a butterfly, this scene comes closest to assessing Guildenstern's position, refusing to admit that he searches for an unverifiable truth which can be apprehended neither intellectually nor intuitively. As he says, "The scientific approach to the examination of phenomena is a defense against the pure emotion of fear" (17), but neither reason nor emotion can provide the answers to keep the existential terror at bay, and the protagonists finally succumb to their fate as it was preordained, not by a god, but by Shakespeare (the playwright behind this playwright).

Guildenstern also considers another possibility to account for his ill luck, that "time has stopped dead" (16), a characteristic of absurdism, but also a dramatic possibility unique to this play and Stoppard's technique. By being rooted in Hamlet, Rosencrantz underscores the ordinariness of the characters and their tangential relationship to any real significance, pointing out the metadramatic aspect of the work, suggesting Shakespeare's vision of life as a stage, wherein all human beings play roles in a preordained drama. There is, however, no deity behind this play, only another work of art in the control of the dramatist; thus no certainty can be asserted. Life, like intellectual and logical speculation, is a hall of mirrors. Art mirrors nature, and as demonstrated here, nature mirrors art, and the two protagonists can only surrender to their inevitable dénouement. As the Player observes, "We do on stage the things that are supposed to happen off. Which is a sort of integrity, if you look on every exit being an entrance somewhere else" (28). Thus, Stoppard carries logic to absurd extremes by questioning whether the character or the play came first, and whether they in turn create new plays without the intermediary playwright. The analogy is to human existence, wherein he examines life as a play in which human action is impossible to define and which creates new dramas whose author is unknowable. Ultimately, what seem to be logic and reason are profoundly flawed, if for no other reason than the existence of Tom Stoppard as the author of Rosencrantz; nonetheless, the work calls into question the significance of existence, the multiple possibilities of interpretation, and makes no definitive statement. As Stoppard has observed, "what I think of as being my distinguishing mark is an absolute lack of certainty about almost anything. So I tend to write about oppositions, rather than heroes. . . ." [14] The play, therefore, introduces most of Stoppard's major concerns, exploring levels of reality and modes of perception through a conflict of ideologies while remaining objective and drawing no conclusions.

The following year, 1967, Stoppard produced Albert's Bridge, a short work which examines relativity and perspective from an Einsteinian basis. Written for radio, as so many of his shorter works are, this play concerns a philosophy graduate whose intellectualizations bring him into sharp conflict with the ordinary mechanics and realities of life. He flees complexity and uncertainty for his position on the bridge, where he has a definite place and a definite task; from this distance, society seems orderly and functional. But ironically, he cannot escape into this artificial perspective, for 1800 men march onto the bridge, and Albert is caught in the collapse of his artificial structure, destroyed by the humanity he sought to escape. Enter a Free Man (1968) is a stage adaptation of Stoppard's first television play, A Walk on the Water (1963), and is one of his most traditionally realistic works. Clearly an apprentice work, the play bears the distinct influence of Bolt and Miller, which Stoppard recognizes, but still introduces his prototypical protagonist. George Riley, an ordinary dreamer, vainly tries to fulfill his credo: "A man must resist. A man must stand apart, make a clean break on his own

two feet! Faith is the key—faith in oneself."15
Caught in a circular predicament, the "free" man lives
a life of illusion and subjective perception. His wife
Constance, whom he calls Persephone, indeed lives in
another world, as both her names suggest, and his
reality seldom impinges upon hers. If reason and
objective, shared reality triumph at the conclusion,
Stoppard suggests their ascendancy can only be at the
expense of freedom.

Stoppard's next work, produced the same year, is
The Real Inspector Hound, a more characteristic and
less traditional play. Bearing a strong resemblance
to the farces of Joe Orton, the work is a slight comedy, but one which advances some of the concerns he
first experimented with in Rosencrantz. Like the
earlier work, it contains an internal play, and again
Stoppard explores the layers of reality by means of the
metadramatic metaphor as the external play merges with
the internal one and creates yet another dramatic work.
A parody of the typical Agatha Christie murder mystery,
the drama lightly examines the difficulty of knowing
identity and the difficulty of assigning personality.
While nothing is as it appears to be, his characters
are unable to determine or verify anything absolutely
through the exercise of empirical reasoning. Much the
same sort of situation is at the heart of After
Magritte (1970), a work which Stoppard maintains is
"not an intellectual play, it's a nuts-and-bolts comedy" (7). Its basic premise is the relativity of
perception in a setting that owes much to The Caretaker
and a situation indebted to The American Dream. The
opening tableau, which shows Mother covered with a bath
towel reclining on an ironing board, Thelma crawling on
all fours in a ball gown, and Reginald in waders blow-
ing on a light bulb, seems to be a typically absurdist
configuration as in Ionesco, or as the title suggests,
in the manner of the surrealist painter Magritte. But
the reader's expectation is soon undercut by a per-
fectly rational explanation for this seemingly bizarre
scene. The entire play is constructed of a series of
his "ambushes," which reveal that truth, like reality,
is solely a matter of perspective. What appears to be
a surreal work is actually a rational exposition of the
nature of surrealism. Somewhat ironically, Thelma can
say, "There's no need to use language. That's what I
always say." 16 In this play, what is said is as open
to misunderstanding as what is perceived. What may
have been a footballer, and old man in pajamas, or a
felon in a surgical mask playing hopscotch, who was

carrying either a football, a tortoise, or a handbag, as well as an ivory cane, or a white stick, or a cricket bat, is actually Inspector Foot in shaving cream, carrying his wife's handbag and parasol, with both legs tangled in his pajama trousers. Nothing is more probable than anything else, and what one perceives is completely subjective. The ambiguity of the title signals Stoppard's method, for the play is "after" Magritte both in the sense of an imitation and as an extension beyond basic surrealistic principles.

Stoppard's second major dramatic success came in 1972 with Jumpers, a play which he maintains "reflects my belief that all political acts have a moral basis to them and are meaningless without it" (12). The play concerns the desire for verification and dramatizes this need as operating on several levels of subjective reality. George Moore, Professor of Moral Philosophy, finds himself to be the last Christian humanist in a society rapidly being controlled and seduced by Sir Archibald Jumper and the Radical Liberals, proponents of materialism and pragmatism. Proceeding from the question, "Are God?" (25), in an attempt to cover both the deity of creation and the deity of goodness, George attempts to come to terms with his own faith and doubts against a background of absolute relativity. Dictating to his secretary, but constantly interrupted throughout the play, he early begins to pose his central question:

> In practice, people admit a Creator to give authority to moral values, and admit moral values to give point to the Creation. But when we place the existence of God within the discipline of a philosophical inquiry, we find these two independent mysteries: the how and the why of the overwhelming question:--
> DOTTY (off): Is anybody there?
> GEORGE (pause): Perhaps all mystical experience is a form of coincidence. Or vice versa, of course. (26)

The sort of qualification, ambiguity, and coincidence is the hallmark of the play, but rather than being simply a display of the playwright's pyrotechnics, this is the substance of a genuine line of philosophical inquiry in itself. Both of the Moores, and Bones as well, attempt to discover a source of faith, but are constantly blocked by accident, chance, and the uses and distortions of reason that impede faith and belief.

Of the pair, Dotty's crisis is the more social and immediate. In the surrealistic opening of the play, which is in fact Dotty's party to celebrate the Rad Lib

victory in the recent elections but is cast as a caba-
ret revue, she is introduced as "the much-missed,
much-loved star of the musical stage, the incomparable,
magnetic Dorothy Moore!" (17). Unable to sing since
all her songs run together in references to the moon,
she is followed by a strip-tease by her husband's
"poker-faced" secretary and fiancee of the soon-to-
be-murdered Duncan McFee, her husband's opponent in the
upcoming debate for which George is preparing his
remarks. Following this bit of stage business is a
performance by the Jumpers, a group of "Logical posi-
tivists, mainly, with a linguistic analyst or two, a
couple of Benthamite Utilitarians . . . lapsed Kantians
and empiricists generally . . . and of course the usual
Behaviourists . . . a mixture of the more philosophical
numbers of the university gymnastics team and the more
gymnastic members of the Philosophy School" (50-51).
As if this display were not incredible in itself, Dotty
can complain, "Get me someone unbelievable!" and "I
have a complaint. These people are supposed to be
incredible and I'm not even astonished. I am not
faintly surprised" (18-19). Dotty has lost her faith
and desperately wants something to believe (and disbe-
lieve) in; the symbol of her career and subject matter
of much of her material, the moon, has lost its primacy. She, and the world, has seen television coverage
of the first moon landing and the abandonment of Astro-
naut Oates by Captain Scott on the lunar surface
because the disabled ship could carry only one person
(22-23). This display of self-serving pragmatism and
absolute reality destroyed the romantic notions she
held about the moon:

> When they first landed, it was as though I'd seen a unicorn on the tele-
> vision news. . . . It was very interesting, of course. But it certainly
> spoiled unicorns. . . . I tried to explain it to the analyst when every-
> body in sight was asking me what was the matter. . . . "What's the
> matter, darling?" . . . "What happened, baby?" What could I say? I came
> over funny at work so I went home early. . . . So it stopped right then
> and there, and in a way my retirement was the greatest triumph of my
> career. . . . They thought it was overwork or alcohol, but it was just
> those little grey men in goldfish bowls, clumping about in their lead
> boots on the television news; it was very interesting, but it certainly
> spoiled that Juney old moon; and much else besides. . . . (39)

Faced with a technological reality on a screen in her
bedroom, she can no longer deny reason:

> Well, it's all over now. Not only are we no longer the still centre of
> God's universe, we're not even uniquely graced by his footprint in man's

image. . . . Man is on the Moon, his feet on solid ground, and he has seen us whole, all in one, little--local . . . and all our absolutes, the thou-shalts and the thou-shalt-nots that seemed to be the very condition of our existence, how did they look to two moonmen with a single neck to save between them? (75)

When a gunshot is the response to her early lament that "Jumpers I've had--yellow, I've had them all! Incredible, barely credible, credible and all too bloody likely--When I say jump, jump!" (20), Stoppard has established the central question of the play as well, for the murderer of McFee is ultimately as unprovable as Dotty's moon or George's God.

Throughout the play, George grapples with his own dilemma: "Does, for the sake of argument, God, so to speak, exist?" (27), for as he points out, both his solace and his despair come from the fact that "When I push my convictions to absurdity, I arrive at God . . ." (67-68). In his attempts to justify the "First Cause," he argues that "a supernatural or divine origin is the logical consequence of the assumption that one thing leads to another, and that this series must have had a first term . . ." (27). He uses such props as a bow and arrow and a tortoise and a hare to try to refute the logic of Zeno, asserting that simply because it has no end, infinity does not necessarily lack a beginning. From this premise, he asserts that,

There is reason and there is cause and there is motion, each in infinite regress towards a moment of origin and a point of ultimate reference--and one day!--as we stare into the fire at the mouth of our cave, suddenly! in an instant of grateful terror, we get it!--the one and only, sufficient unto himself, outside the action, uniquely immobile!--the Necessary Being, the First Cause, the Unmoved Mover!! (28-29)

What George--as well as Dotty and Bones--wants to prove is unprovable; he gets far too enmeshed in the nature of philosophic inquiry, in such distinctions and qualifications as those between "knowledge in the sense of having-experience-of, with knowledge in the sense of being-acquainted-with, and knowledge in the sense of inferring facts with knowledge in the sense of comprehending truths," to which Dotty adds "knowing in the biblical sense of screwing" (36).

As a philosopher, George deals in ideas; Dotty flatly tells him that "You're living in dreamland!" (31). At the same time, he is keenly aware of the fallibility of language to convey thought and, in both

his and Dotty's cases, leap of faith judgements. His
confusion arises largely from the fact that "language
is an approximation of meaning and not a logical symbolism for it" (24), and "Words betray the thoughts
they are supposed to express. Even the most generalized truth begins to look like special pleading as soon
as you trap it in language" (46). He is aware of the
problem in his reasoning but is at the same time, like
Dotty, helpless to do anything about it:

> The study of moral philosophy is an attempt to determine what we mean
> when we say that something is good and that something else is bad. Not
> all value judgements, however, are the proper study of the moral philoso-
> pher. Language is a finite instrument crudely applied to an infinity of
> ideas, and one consequence of the failure to take account of this is that
> modern philosophy has made itself ridiculous by analyzing such statements
> as "This is a good bacon sandwich," or "Bedser has a good wicket." (63)

Therefore, George's problem is essentially the same as
Dotty's, Bones', and the reader's: how to wring from
language verifiable truth, and within its impossibility
lies the answer to this question. Nothing is verifiable and nothing can be known absolutely; reason provides no aid to those who ask unanswerable questions.
In the Coda, which is cast in "bizarre dream form"
(83), George asserts that "nothing is certain" and
breaks down into nonsense, asking the readers, as
"gentlemen of the jury, to consider the testimony of
such witnesses as Zeno Evil, St. Thomas Augustine,
Jesus Moore and my late friend the late Herr Thumper
who was as innocent as a rainbow . . ." (87).

Both the Moores are, in different ways, responding
to the philosophy of the Rad Libs, voiced most often by
Sir Archibald Jumper. George's efforts are an attempt
to answer the philosophy of the slain McFee, the voice
of "Orthodox mainstream" (49) belief:

> He thinks good and bad aren't actually good and bad in any absolute or
> metaphysical sense, he believes them to be categories of our own making,
> social and psychological conventions which we have evolved in order to
> make living in groups a practical possibility, in much the same way as we
> have evolved the rules of tennis without which Wimbledon Fortnight would
> be a complete shambles, do you see? (48)

McFee's paper further asserts that "goodness, whether
in men or music, depends on your point of view. By
discrediting the idea of beauty as an aesthetic absolute, he hopes to discredit by associatin the idea of
goodness as a moral absolute and as a first step he

directs us to listen to different kinds of music" (53), which, coincidentally, have been playing as appropriate background music to Dotty's meeting with Bones. George asserts that "The irreducible fact of goodness is not implicit in one kind of action any more than in its opposite, but in the existence of a relationship between the two. It is the sense of comparisons being in order" (55). Reason, as George understands it, is incapable of conquering the pragmatism of Archie. Dotty repeats the Vice Chancellor's stance:

> There's no question of things getting better. Things are one way or they are another; "better" is how we see them, Archie says, and I don't personally, very much; though sometimes he makes them seem not so bad after all—no, that's wrong, too: he knows not "seems." Things do no seem, on the one hand, they are; and on the other hand, bad is not what they can be. . . . Things and actions, you understand, can have any number of real and verifiable properties. But good and bad, better and worse, these are not real properties of things, they are just expressions of our feelings about them. (41)

Therefore, George's question, "How the hell does one know what to believe?" (71), is unanswerable by the very bases of his own arguments. One assigns belief subjectively in a leap of faith decision, not through the use of reason, for coincidence rules in the play, and language only faultily conveys meaning and can be easily manipulated. For example, Archie turns his verbal powers to George's basic question, distorting the moral philosopher's meanings through the use of reason:

> GEORGE: It occurred to you that belief in God and the conviction that God doesn't exist amount to much the same thing?
> ARCHIE: It gains from careful phrasing. Religious faith and atheism differ mainly about God; about Man they are in accord: Man is the highest form of life, he has duties he has rights, etcetera, and it is usually better to be kind than cruel. Even if there is some inscrutable divinity behind it all, our condition for good or ill is apparently determined by our choice of actions, and choosing seems to be a genuine human possibility. Indeed, it is surely religious zeal rather than atheism which is historically notorious in the fortunes of mankind. (68)

While Stoppard cannot be seen as an advocate of Archie's cold pragmatism, his display of the failure of both faith and reason suggests that, together, George's humanism and Archie's insistence on the primacy of choice would be a viable alternative to the polarities represented by the individuals in the play. Couch

65

describes his mentor McFee as wavering, like Dotty, in his belief after having witnessed the display on the moon; logical positivism cannot admit altruism, and the Professor of Logic announced, "I have seen the future . . . and it's yellow" (80), the color of the Rad Libs.

The decision to recant logical positivism that would have led McFee into a monastery was in reaction to the philosophy behind Archie's brutal assessment of reality: "The truth to us philosophers . . . is always an interim judgement. We will never even know for certain who did shoot McFee. Unlike mystery novels, life does not guarantee a denouement; and if it came, how would one know whether to believe it?" (81). Closing the play on this thought, Stoppard seems to condemn pragmatism as well as George's desire for verification. One can only choose and act upon what one believes to be true, for reality is subjective, and action in the face of contingency is the only viable postmodern stance. Speculation, either philosophic or romantic, is inextricably tied to language, which, as the play demonstrates, is a faulty medium of communication to convey truth. Without a notion of subjective reality, one may accept the brutal but realistic assessment of present reality offered by Archie at the end of the Coda:

> Do not despair--many are happy much of the time; more eat than starve, more are healthy than sick, more curable than dying; not so many dying as dead; and one of the thieves was saved. Hell's bells and all's well-- half of the world is at peace with itself, and so is the other half; vast areas are unpolluted; millions of children grow up without suffering deprivation, and millions, while deprived, grow up without suffering cruelties, and millions, while deprived and cruelly treated, none the less grow up. No laughter is sad and many tears are joyful. (87)

Without individual action, a collective mentality will perpetuate this condition; therefore, the Coda of Jumpers is a warning after an ending that states and demonstrates that all truth is relative to individual perception.

The isolation in the Moore marriage, as each partner struggles with the loss of faith in a separate section of the house, and their opposition to logical positivism result in a chaos of philosophical stances reflected in the chaotic, episodic nature of the plot. Ideas jump about in the play just as the Jumpers literally do. The actions and the dialogue both reflect intellectual gynmastics, leaps in flawed reasoning and faith, and jumps in false logic. On all its levels, the play demonstrates the inadequacy of language to convey the multiplicity of modern existence where absolutes do not exist. While Stoppard may have sympathy with George, the protagonists' stance is as unviable as any other in the work, which is a demonstration of the multiplicity of systems for dealing with existence and the relativity of perception. The playwright remains objective and demands that readers subjectively impose their own order on the farce.

Eminently theatrical with its ostensibly absurdist opening scene--complete with acrobats, a murder, and a stripper--the play undercuts the expectations immediately presented by being a serious discussion of philosophical points of view. The play mingles comedy and tragedy, as in the deaths of the animals, employs expressionistic properties, such as the giant television and the dermatograph, and concludes with the surrealistic Coda. The effect is at once farcical in the juxtaposition of methods and techniques, and serious, for that very juxtaposition becomes an argument of the play--philosophy and intellectual jumping are postmodern realities.

Aesthetics replace philosophy in Stoppard's next play, Travesties (1974), which Stoppard believes "asks whether the words 'revolutionary' and 'artist' are capable of being synonymous, or whether they are mutually exclusive, or something in between" (11). The play dramatizes the conjunction of a variety of styles and philosophies, both aesthetic and political, at a time of revolution, both literal and metaphorical. It takes place, for the most part, in the memory of Henry Carr, a minor bureaucrat in the British embassy in Zurich during World War I, and the action of the play is subject to the subjectivity and malleability of Carr's perceptions and recall. Although the figures who populate Carr's memory are stellar--Joyce, Lenin, and Tzara--the first level of concern is with Carr himself. A typical Stoppard protagonist, he is an ordinary and undistinguished man, important only for being a minor character in Ulysses (for having offended Joyce) and for the accident of his proximity to greatness. Carr finds himself poised in the center of a triangle of oppositions. Joyce represents the aesthetic artist who believes in art for art's sake; he is a father of modernism, an aesthetic revolution, and is the subject of Carr's wounded pride. The bourgeoise nonentity, Carr, therefore stands in direct opposition to Joyce. Fancying himself something of an artist, Carr is hardest on Joyce and Tzara as his memory alters and distorts (or travesties) them in a variety of forms. Lenin alone receives direct and realistic treatment in the play, which many critics have found to be a weakness, but the character, as in the plays of Pinter and Albee, is a touchstone of objective reality, against which one can measure the corruptive power of Carr's subjective perceptions.

While Stoppard provides a variety of interpretations of the nature of art and revolution, none of them gains his explicit approval. His position as playwright and the basis of the drama in Wilde's comedy suggest that his sympathies would most appropriately be seen as aligned with Joyce. Perhaps the only valid and generally acceptable definition of art comes from Carr: "An artist is someone who is gifted in some way that enables him to do something more or less well which can only be done badly or not at all by someone who is not thus gifted." [17] This definition embraces Joyce's aestheticism, Tzara's nihilism, as well as Lenin's political ability. But of the difference between art and politics, Stoppard suggests that while both a Lenin and a Joyce are artists, their abilities to affect objective reality are quite different. Carr says that "For every thousand people there's nine hundred doing the work, ninety doing well, nine doing good, and one lucky bastard who's the artist" (46). This description fits all four men, for as Carr also points out, "to be an artist at all is like living in Switzerland during a world war" (38). The true distinction between aesthetics and politics is evident in the opposition of Joyce and Lenin. Joyce says that "An artist is the magician put among men to gratify--capriciously--their urge for immortality" (62), and of his Ulysses and its basis in The Odyssey, he concludes: "it is a theme so overwhelming that I am almost afraid to treat it. And yet I with my Dublin Odyssey will double that immortality, yes by God there's a corpse that will dance for some time yet and leave the world precisely as it finds it . . ." (62-63). Art, clearly, does not change objective reality. Lenin voices the same concerns from his political viewpoint in discussing the effect of Beethoven's Appassionata:

It always makes me feel, perhaps naively, it makes me feel proud of the miracles that human beings can perform. But I can't listen to music often. It affects my nerves, makes me want to say nice stupid things and pat the heads of those people who while living in this vile hell can

68

create such beauty. Nowadays we can't pat heads or we'll get our hands
bitten off. We've got to <u>hit</u> heads, hit them without mercy, though
ideally we're against doing violence to people . . . Hm, one's duty is
infernally hard. . . . (89)

Politics subsume aesthetics, for apparently the way to
alter the world is not through art.

The aesthetics that are the subject of the play are
reflected in its form as well. The travesties of the
title certainly suggest the damage done to history and
the characters of Joyce, Lenin, and Tzara by Carr's
memory, and Stoppard's dramatic technique reflects that
damage in the parodic presentation of these characters.
But the travesty is also to Wilde's play, reflected in
the appropriation of his basic plot, some of his
characters, and his epigramatic dialogue. Just as art
cannot reflect the true concerns of objective reality,
the stylized comedic dialogue in the play betrays the
seriousness of its message. Again employing the
resources of the theater, Stoppard creates a farce
wedded to the drama of ideas in a work that John
William Cooke argues "is not formless, but in its
excess of forms, the play challenges perceivers to
become makers themselves, and thereby exalts the efficacy of the imagination while questioning the locus of
truth."[18]

Since his discussion of politics in <u>Travesties</u>,
Stoppard's drama has become more political in nature.
His <u>Dirty Linen</u> (1975) is a light comedy about sexual
indiscretions in Parliament, a linguistic farce reminiscent of Restoration comedy. Early regarded as
apolitical, Stoppard commented:

there are political plays which are about specific situations, and there
are political plays which are about a general political situation, and
there are plays which are <u>political acts</u> in themsleves, insofar as it can
be said that attacking or insulting an audience is a political act (and
it <u>is</u> said). (12)

Even in his recent work, however, he has yet to attempt
this third category, while <u>Dirty Linen</u> does seem to
indicate an interest in the first two.

While in 1968 Stoppard could state: "I burn with
no cause. I cannot say that I write with any social
objective,"[19] three of his more recent plays do
directly confront political issues and abandon the mode
of farce. C. W. E. Bigsby suggests that in his recent

work, Stoppard "is trying to re-establish both the absolute need for moral responsiblity and the necessity to acknowledge language as in some way rationally and morally linked to a world whose reality must be assumed even if it cannot ultimately be proved."[20] Every Good Boy Deserves Favor (1977) is "A Play for Actors and Orchestra" and is the result of a collaboration with André Previn. Although the work breaks the principles of time and space, it is essentially traditional in form and is an elaboration on the metaphor of a sour note in an orchestra transferred to politics. It is a demonstration of the perversion of logic which results in seeming absurdity, as is so much of his work, but this logic is factually reported from contemporary politics and was inspired by the situation of the Russian dissident, Victor Fainberg. Produced the same year, Professional Foul was similarly inspired by the political position of the Czech playwright, Vaclav Havel. Written for television to celebrate Amnesty International's Prisoner of Conscience Year, the play concerns a professor of ethics in Prague for a professional meeting. It demonstrates the variability of justice in a decidedly political context and explores the impossibility of belief in absolute values in a typically Stoppardian vein. Night and Day (1978) is set in a former British colony now controlled by a black dictator modeled after Idi Amin. It is a traditional thesis play that examines the responsibilities of the press and is stylistically distinguished by the two separate manifestations of Ruth, whose thoughts are literalized on stage.

Despite what appears to be a new direction in his more recent work, Stoppard's dramatic canon evinces a distinct postmodern theory. His vision is humanistic, but objective, and rather than being a pessimistic statement about the fragmentation of modern life, his plays celebrate multiplicity. In thematic scope, his works range throughout postmodern philosophy and aesthetics, exploring not only the manifestations of possible choices, but their roots as well. He refuses to make any single statement which might be interpreted as his own personal vision. By creating characters who embody aspects of belief and possible choice, isolated in their own subjective perceptions of reality, he dramatizes the conflict of ideologies, reflecting the postmodern obsession with ideas.

The effect his works have on their readers and audience is closely aligned with the basic principles of Epic Theater. Pointedly intellectual, as Brecht demanded a play must be in order to inspire its viewer to conscious cerebral response, Stoppard's works engage by being eminently theatrical and comedic, while dealing with intensely serious subject matter which must be individually apprehended and digested intellectually. If Thomas R. Whitaker's assertion, "a play's meaning must include the meaning of our participation in its playing,"[21] is taken as a criterion of post-McLuhan drama, Stoppard serves his age by demanding a subjective response from his reader. His metadramatic stance, which suggests that life is not particularly different from the nature of drama, questions the nature, and authorship, of the play of existence. The reader becomes both audience and conspirator in the life of the play. The seeming absurdity of many of his plots, paradoxically grounded in an insistence on logic and reason, distances the reader from easy identification with the work. One is confronted with a plurality of choices, not solutions, and like the characters, readers must construct their own means of coming to terms with objective reality in order to assimilate the play, as well as to cope with their own forms of objective reality.

Joan FitzPatrick Dean maintains that Stoppard distances himself, not his audience, from his work and that his "brand of 'distance' from his characters is antithetical to the celebrated 'distancing' of Bertolt Brecht's Verfremsdungeffect as well as the autobiographical or confessional impulse that fuels the metafictionists."[22] But the effect is decidedly similar, and the technique is not as different as Dean indicates. In his three major plays, he includes the epic devices of song and documentary (Jumpers and Travesties), a detached narrator (Travesties), montage and anti-naturalistic character presentation (Rosencrantz, Jumpers, and Travesties). And the epic impulse behind much of his overt theatricality is also grounded in absurdist technique. His lack of linear development creates an episodic dramatic action, his staging calls for heightened unreality and universality of minimalism, and his dialogue evinces the absurdists' distrust of the communicative power of language. His combination of epic and absurdist methods is highly individual, for his primary concern is with realism, the levels of subjective reality which characterize the interior nature of postmodern drama.

Through externalized thought, the literalization of

the figurative, and the presentation of the multiplicity of objective reality, he achieves the effect of
exploring the individual consciousness as it is subjectively perceived. He does not rely on the shifts from
external to internal reality as do Pinter and Albee,
but immediately plunges his reader into a situation
that seems chaotic. His protagonists are ordinary,
undistinguished people who attempt to come to terms
with life against the background of importance, against
which the reader is invited to measure them, and all of
the conceptions of reality manifested in the plays are
valid; they are simply in disharmony, creating much of
the comedy in his work. The technique of montage
emphasizes the essential loneliness of the individual
and the difficulty of communication as well as the
interior nature of reality--the existential reality of
postmodern existence. His characters never connect
with each other, and while Stoppard himself may feel
that salvation and integration may lie in transcendent
values, he most often concludes with his characters as
isolated as they began. They can probe their own memories and compare their perceptions with those of
others, but unlike Albee, Stoppard does not insist on
the stripping away of insulating illusions. His only
mandate is that the individual must live a moral life
and be true to self; one must attempt an integrated
consciousness from an individual perspective. Unfortu-
nately, the playwright observes, the tools for compre-
hension and verification are severely flawed: neither
faith nor logic is operable in a world with so many
conflicting impulses.

Like his mentors, Stoppard attempts to render a new
and accurate vision of existence in dramatic form.
Like Eliot, he is possessed of negative capability,
arguing for a stoic acceptance of the unknown in the
face of contingency, and like Joyce, he celebrates the
multiplicity of the ordinary, reproducing the shifts
and flows of a subjectively apprehended consciousness.
His work is self-consciously literary, alluding to
masterpieces in all genres from classicism to modernism, providing a "moral matrix" for an enlightened and
intellectually aware readership.

Notes

[1] Beyond Absurdity: The Plays of Tom Stoppard (Cranbury, NJ: Associated Univ.
Presses, 1979), pp. 153-57.

[2] Quoted in Kenneth Tynan, "Withdrawing with Style from the Chaos," in Show People: Profiles in Entertainment (New York: Simon and Schuster, 1979), p. 46.

[3] "Count Zero Splits the Infinitive: Tom Stoppard's Plays," Encounter, 45, No. 5 (Nov. 1975), p. 70.

[4] "Ambushes for the Audience: Towards a High Comedy of Ideas," Theatre Quarterly, 4 (1974), 6; subsequent references to this profile will appear as page numbers in parentheses in the text.

[5] Quoted in Tynan, p. 102.

[6] Tynan, p. 57.

[7] Quoted in Tynan, p. 64.

[8] Tom Stoppard (New York: Frederick Ungar, 1981), p. 49.

[9] Tom Stoppard, Rosencrantz and Guildenstern Are Dead (New York: Grove, 1967), p. 21; subsequent references to this edition will appear as page numbers in parentheses in the text.

[10] Quoted in Tynan, p. 61.

[11] Quoted in Tynan, p. 100.

[12] "Tom Stoppard's Jumpers: The Separation from Reality," Bulletin of the West Virginia Association of College English Teachers, 2 (1975), 49.

[13] Tom Stoppard, Jumpers (New York: Grove, 1972), p. 78; subsequent references to this edition will appear as page numbers in parentheses in the text.

[14] Quoted in Ronald Hayman, Tom Stoppard, 2nd ed. (London: Heinemann, 1978), p. 40.

[15] Tom Stoppard, Albert's Bridge, in Albert's Bridge and Other Plays (New York: Grove, 1977), p. 16.

[16] Tom Stoppard, After Magritte, in The Real Inspector Hound and After Magritte (New York: Grove, 1975), p. 69.

[17] Tom Stoppard, Travesties (New York: Grove, 1975), p. 38; subsequent references to this edition will appear as page numbers in parentheses in the text.

[18] "The Optical Allusion: Perception and Form in Stoppard's Travesties," Modern Drama, 24, No. 4 (Dec. 1981), p. 525.

[19] Quoted in Tynan, p. 48.

[20] C. W. E. Bigsby, "The Language of Crisis in British Theatre: The Drama of Cultural Pathology," in Contemporary English Drama, ed. C. W. E. Bigsby (New York: Holmes and Meier, 1981), p. 26.

[21] Fields of Play in Modern Drama (Princeton: Princeton Univ. Press, 1977), p. 31.

[22] Tom Stoppard: Comedy as a Moral Matrix (Columbia: Univ. of Missouri Press, 1981), p. 106.

74

FIVE: SAM SHEPARD
Emotional Renegade

Parallel in impulse but opposite in form, Sam
Shepard stands as an American counterpoint to the
British Stoppard. Unlike Stoppard's drama, which draws
on established dramatic traditions, is self-consciously
intellectual, and is accessible within a recognizable
framework, Shepard's canon is highly individualistic,
pre-intellectual, and intensely subjective in both form
and scope. Elusive and difficult to assess, his work
is often discussed in hyperbolic generalization, and
few scholars or critics have been willing to penetrate
far below the surface, preferring instead to praise
Shepard's visceral intensity and bestow upon him the
hope of promise which had fallen to Edward Albee a
generation earlier. While his work may "constitute a
series of facets of a single continuing act of imagination," as Richard Gilman asserts,[1] and his methods hold
much promise for revivifying an increasingly commercial
native theater, Shepard's drama is neither as apocalyptic in vision nor as intensely American as most criticism would suggest.

Gilman observes that "Shepard seems to have come
out of no literary or theatrical tradition at all but
precisely from the breakdown or absence--on the level
of art if not of commerce--of all such traditions in
America" (xi), which is true on one level; where Albee
had begun to experiment in new voices and forms, Shepard presents a unified dramatic vision that borrows
much from his predecessors but cannot be viewed as
derivative. His is the first totally postmodern voice
in American drama. On the broadest level, his themes
are "the death (or betrayal) of the American dream; the
decay of our national myths; the growing mechanization
of our lives; the search for roots; the travail of the
family," but as Gilman observes, these are the same
themes of the late modern playwrights (ix), and rather
than being expressly national, these are the concerns
of contemporary society, not just America. Michael

Early maintains that "Shepard is a true American primitive," and, like many other critics, sees him in the
line of descent from Emerson and Whitman. He explains
that "even though Shepard is one of our most modernist
playwrights--his indulgent surrealism being just one
example--what he more keenly resembles is a transcen-
dentalist or new romantic whose 'innocent eye' wonders
at all it surveys and records experience without cen-
sure."[2] To the extent that he is an American working
from a native perspective and incorporating elements of
native consciousness, Shepard can be seen as nationalistic, but an insistence on this perspective obscures
his contribution to postmodern drama.

As a result of his generation (he was born in 1943)
and his cultural milieu (early moving from Illinois to
Southern California), much of Shepard's vision has been
shaped by the beats of the 1950s and the pop culture of
the 60s and 70s. Characteristic of Shepard is his
sense of displacement and isolation, an existential
awareness of homelessness and meaninglessness. He
insists on the objects, the trappings, of a postmodern
existence rather than the philosophy which informs
them. To him, the individual is a spiritual tabula
rasa, wandering in a world dominated by the tyranny of
things as symbols of subjectively apprehended significance. Like Albee, Shepard is an outsider dispassion-
ately recording the signs and symbols of contemporary
existence in a culture whose values have become empty
and hollow. His technique is to ransack native myth to
create a new and viable system of symbology and belief.
His territory is in the open stretches of the West and
Midwest and his characters are the culturally displaced, the quintessential cowboy, the rock star, the
refugee from the city. He does possess what Robert Coe
labels a "deeply ingrained Western sense of psychological rootlessness and space,"[3] but only as the postmodern existential quester possesses the same sense.
His inverted mythic structure collapses time into a
single moment, echoing Four Quartets and Proust, but in
a highly individualistic way. The Shepard hero is
often a conflation of the cowboy and the rock star who
functions in an almost surreal version of the near
future. His "Cowboy Mouth" is a symbol of the past,
present, and future embodied in one displaced person.

Like those of Samuel Beckett, many of Shepard's
plays center on paired characters who journey out to
face the unknown together and represent the two halves
of a divided self, but unlike Vladimir and Estragon, or

Rosencrantz and Guildenstern, "paired existence is not shared existence, at least not for very long in Shepard," as Ren Frutkin observes.[4] Represented as the archetypal figures of the cowboy and his sidekick, his heroes must individually confront and subjectively order the menace or terror they encounter as they perceive it, for Shepard is primarily concerned with the individual in isolation. Also, Shepard writes almost exclusively about male experience, a dramatic condition for which he has been faulted by feminists. Florence Falk asserts that "Shepard never explicitly says that his vision of an America overrun by a horde of renegade cowboys, and their women, trailing at heel, is a distinctly national pathology or whether it reaches beyond, to tell us something that pertains in general to the human condition."[5] However, few of Shepard's metaphors are localized, and like most postmodern dramatists, he never provides facile solutions or analyses.

The dramatic impulses which inform his plays are almost preconscious, for like most postmodern dramas, they are imagistic associations of events which suggest dream states; they deny cause and effect like Stoppard's works, but without relying on any exercise of reason. This associational, and almost surreal, structure provokes scholars to conclude, as does Bruce W. Powe, that the playwright's intentions "are visceral rather than intellectual, moody rather than political."[6] He strives for the effect of spontaneity and roughness, for such is the nature of the experience he attempts to communicate. More than intellectual stimulation of his audience, he strives to achieve an emotional response that will in turn lead to self-conscious meditation.

Like Bertold Brecht, he relies heavily on song and monologue, roles constructed not to reveal character but to promote a sense of performance, and many of the visual pyrotechnics of theatricality. Like the principles of Epic Theater, Shepard's technique is designed to elicit an immediate response from the reader/audience who is not seduced into an easy identification with the play, but the reaction is emotional rather than intellectual as Brecht advocated. The viewer is assaulted on a subconscious, emotional level and drawn into the experience of the play (clearly the result of Shepard's close association with contemporary performance theoreticians); like the characters, the reader must individually and subjectively apprehend the play

and process it. The play's success lies in the reader's ability to render emotion into thought, thereby
assigning meaning to the work.

Addressing himself to Shepard's early works, which
are clearly experimental, Michael Bloom concludes that,

> as with much of the writing of this time, Shepard's work is itself an
> attack on the objective, rational apprehension of knowledge. The
> apocalyptic proceeds by dreams, visions, and hallucinations. Given the
> anti-rationalist method of the apocalyptic vision, it is clear why real-
> ism with its rational, objective vision of reality, held no interest for
> Shepard in the early part of his career. [7]

As in Pinter, traditional realism in not totally
excluded, for it often provides the framework from
which Shepard's dramatic action departs and is
measured. One of the most apocalyptic of his works,
Icarus's Mother, has an objectively presented opening
in its picnic setting but quickly moves to defy expectation in its stylized presentation of events. Bonnie
Marranca observes that "Shepard is an abstract expressionist in the theatre, emotionalizing simultaneously
several planes of reality which flow together in a
spontaneous outpouring of feelings." [8] Both in method
and structure, Shepard's treatment of realism is in
direct line of evolution from the traditional mode of
memory or subjective presentation in A Glass Menagerie
through Beckett to postmodernism, as in Travesties.
True reality in Shepard is individually perceived, and
as in Stoppard, multiple versions of subjective, existential reality operate simultaneously within the play.
His plays locate the reality of human existence internally in a set of subjectively perceived and ordered
events, creating a dramatic objective correlative.

Therefore, the immediate effect of Shepard's drama
is identical to that of Stoppard's: the plays are
pastiches of different styles and modes that can slip
from traditional, representational reality to personal
hallucination on the most subjective level without
disrupting the overall structure. Emphasizing their
essential isolation and the interiority of their existences, characters perceive no more or less than they
choose, and they act subjectively in a dramatic world
where motives are not as important as the fact that
action, or choice, exists. The events are arranged
episodically, but unlike in Stoppard's technique, which
is based on extensions of logic, Shepard's scenes are
connected by the act of perception, linked by stream of

consciousness rather than reason, thus reflecting dramatically the workings of the individual mind. Dramatic movement and development have the immediate compulsion of the dream state and are designed to illustrate the individual mind perceiving its own consciousness, operating according to unarticulated and self-defined dicta. The presence of more than one character further layers the structure to the point that a seeming clash of styles symbolizes the clash of personalities and values, no one of which is shown to be any more real than any other, for the dramatist maintains an intensely objective stance to his creations. More so than his predecessors, Shepard tends to truncate his plays at the moment traditionally perceived as crisis or climax, throwing into doubt not only what the resolution may be, but the authenticity and verifiability of what precedes the particular climactic moment. Because he creates his symbols to function on a preconscious level, the plays have an immediate and emotional impact; because they defy facile dismissal on this level, the works demand subjective evaluation by the reader, thus ultimately encouraging an intellectual engagement on the part of the reader untouched since the experiments of the first masters of the avant garde early in the twentieth-century.

The array of characters who populate these dramas contributes to this distance/identification effect by actually dramatizing the same quality. Shepard's characters are always aware of their roles as actors, for the playwright continues to dramatize the contemporary individual's role as actor in a largely incomprehensible drama unfolding around him. The characters tend to favor the monologue as a means of expression, suggesting both their self-consciousness of their existence as artifacts and their own detachment from the action into which they are inexplicably plunged; they can break role to meditate on what they are experiencing. Stu in Chicago is engaged in one continuous monologue, punctuated occasionally by the necessity of his existence in the action around him, and more naturalistically, most of the characters in Icarus's Mother pause at some time to meditate on the action they are involved in. Shepard's characters possess the sense of being involved with other people while being simultaneously isolated in their individual consciousnesses, contemplating the significance of their own actions and perceptions. The fragmentary apprehension and imperfect understanding of the actions they are involved in suggest the essential loneliness of individuals unable to communicate to the society of which they are a part. Ross Wetzsteon summarizes Shepard's technqiue: "Shepard's theater creates a new vision of space (emotional rather than physical), a new vision of time (immediate rather than continuous), a new vision of character (spontaneous rather than coherent), and a new vision of story (consciousness rather than behavior)."[9]

In terms of his development, an important chronological distinction must be made between Shepard's early drama and his most recent plays. Although a critical and popular success off- and off-off-Broadway, having accumulated several Obie awards early in his career, Shepard began a serious reassessment and refinement of his dramatic style after The Tooth of Crime (1972), the last of his surreal rock and roll plays. Beginning with Geography of a Horse Dreamer (1974), he has worked more in a traditionally realistic style with more emphasis on structure, clearly demonstrating the truly experimental nature of his more than two dozen early works. In the later plays, particularly The Curse of the Starving Class, Buried Child, and True West, he begins to rely more on objective reality as a framework. His attentions are no less focused on individuals and tend to include them within a sealed social grouping, producing a traditionally recognizable dramatic tension and structure. This turning point in his career represents the shift from simply presenting a dramatic experience to dramatizing the same sort of experience.

However, the roots of Shepard's mature accomplishments (if such a term can be anything but fallacious when applied to such a young playwright), lie in the experiments in the first plays. Shepard seems to place an almost ritualistic, incantatory value on language, and style in his plays, of which language forms a large part, is often the substance of the character, if not the action of the entire play, as it is in The Tooth of Crime. He has commented: "I feel that language is a veil holding demons and angels which the characters are always out of touch with. Their quest in the play is the same as ours in life--to find those forces, to meet them face to face and end the mystery."[10] In his later work, language functions in much the same way as it does in Pinter, often as a reflection of inarticulation, but always as the touchstone to an important, but unspoken, subtext. While there is no lack of action in his drama, there is often a level of linguistic action that parallels the physical, enhancing or diminishing the positions of the characters. Music operates similarly in his works, particularly in the rock and roll plays where songs are inserted as integral and Brechtian elements of the text and are often composed by Shepard or by members of the band with which he once played, The Holy Modal Rounders. His stylized use of music and language is frequently more theatrical exploitation than a genuine dramatic device and has been replaced in his later work with less overt techniques for achieving the same range of multiplicity in a more richly evocative technique than collage.

Shepard's dramatic debut was in 1964 at the age of twenty, and by the next year he was writing the plays for which he is most widely known. His Icarus's Mother (1965) is a postmodern parable that points out man's impotence in a technological world where he is continuously threatened with immediate extinction by nuclear holocaust. Within a framework of external reality, his assortment of characters, about whom readers know no more than they can assume from the action, for Shepard provides no antecedent action, go about the business of an afternoon picnic, attempting to make sense of a pilot flying erratically above them, and occasionally lapsing into monologue as they try to interpret the message and intentions of this contemporary Icarus (or rather Icarus' mother, if one interprets the bomb itself as Icarus). Clearly Pinteresque, the play suggests the difficulty of verifying or knowing anything, from the dynamics of the personal social group to the cosmic message of the pilot, which is "$\underline{E}$ equals $\underline{MC}$ squared," [11] the modern representation of the absolute relativity of all things.

In Chicago (1966) Shepard pulls his objective framework in more tightly to focus on the consciousness of his central character, Stu, as he sits in a bathtub while Joy prepares to leave on a trip. Again, no background or motivation is supplied in what is perhaps Shepard's most recognizably absurdist play. Aware of his existence as an actor on a stage, Stu in his bath is the central reality of the play and the other characters are virtually props which represent the wanderings of his consciousness as he moves from the contemplation of a small subjective problem, Joy's departure, to the typically Shepardian "universal problem of man's being civilized to the suffocating point of losing his balls," according to the original director, Ralph Cook.[12] On a set conspicuously bare of

all but the most essential properties, the ordinary
becomes threatening in Stu's inarticulate contemplation
of his own relativity and insignificance. The play is
a dramatization of the individual's sense of existential reality and the fear inherent in such a mode of
consciousness.

In the same year, his Red Cross attempts to represent more imagistically the chaos from which judgements
are made, wherein pre-intellectual, inarticulated
feeling and thought are brought to the edge of reality
and reason without surrendering to them. The playwright is clearly more interested in doing something to
his readers than saying anything to them. But by the
next year, Fourteen Hundred Thousand reverses this
pattern of experimentation, and language becomes more
important than action, which is reduced to simple
geometry, literally in the building of the bookcase and
metaphorically in the description of the futuristic
linear city. His point is to demonstrate the difficulty of communication as each character is lost in a
personal reality, which does not impinge on that of any
other character. Ultimately, the play is a dramatization of isolation, and it is the last significant play
that is clearly derivative, imitating and conflating
the themes and techniques of Pinter and Albee.

A distinctive dramatic voice is clearly evident,
however, in La Turista (1967), which Marranca maintains
"isn't realism or absurdism; it's a kind of actualism
uniquely Shepard's."[13] Suggesting that America is a
source of illness, Act II occurs chronologically before
the Mexican sequence in Act I, and his very American
characters, Kent and Salem (brands of cigarettes),
suffer in both balanced acts (reminiscent of Waiting
for Godot), from an illness suggested by the title. In
this pastiche of American jargon, which suggests both a
despair and a humor, the ruling image is of sickness,
of a sort of joke that kills. The secondary characters
suggest the motif of the mad doctor who creates a
monster, in this case, postmodern man. Although the
play lacks traditional focus and dramatic development,
it is structured by the two balanced acts and is unified through Shepard's use of fragmentary slang mixed
with medical jargon and pat clichés. It attempts to
chart the sources of a modern malaise which takes many
forms, from the Mexican dysentery to the American
sleeping sickness, a life-in-death illness. The medical men in the play attempt to apply science to cure a
disease which the protagonist, Kent, knows cannot be

cured by medicine or magic. Typically, Shepard leaves his conflict unresolved as Kent swings through a wall in escape, leaving only a cartoon outline of his shape behind him, rejecting the external reality of the play; he seeks his own cure within his own sense of subjective reality.

Shepard's Operation Sidewinder (1970) is often viewed as the culmination of his early career, although many of the specific techniques he uses in this work continue to appear in his drama in the early 1970s. While inevitably difficult in the early plays, a summary of this play is virtually impossible due to the wild range of elements it employs: Indian ritual, figures from the drug culture, the Air Force, contemporary science gone mad, the Black Panthers, the SDS, UFOs, a computer in the form of a domesticated snake gone feral, desert prospectors. The play is a collage of native American myths and archetypes juxtaposed against contemporary politics and establishments. The effect of the play belies its chaotic approach, however, for it maintains a credible plot which in itself parodies the multiplicity of contemporary roles and forces which bear on the individual. It actually only slightly exaggerates the possible reality of any one element, effectively dramatizing the possibility of a number of situations simultaneously taken to extremes. It is clearly an artifact of the pop culture but at the same time a serious statement about the mechanization of modern life and the dehumanizing effect such a culture has on its citizens. Man is surrounded by a variety of beliefs and institutions which all work in opposition and are based on special interests, the origins of which are obscure. People can either surrender to the machinations of the modern world or retreat within, where their only possibility of integration and authenticity lies. Of the multifaceted realities which comprise the play and the beliefs which they reflect, Shepard seems sympathetic only to the Spider Lady, the Indian mystic. Significantly, the Indian rituals in the play are the only elements to be presented realistically and seriously and are based on the Spider Lady's prophesy that,

A great war is about to begin. . . . It is only materialistic people who seek to make shelters. Those who are at peace in their own hearts already are in the great shelter of life. . . . The war will be a spiritual conflict with material things. Material matters will be destroyed by spiritual beings who will remain to create one world and one nation under one power, that of the Creator. [14]

At his most apocalyptic, Shepard concludes the play
with a surreal vision, for the spiritually pure Indians
and the purified Honey and Young Man ascend, leaving
the chaos of contemporary existence behind them. The
implications of the ascension are left unclear, for
Shepard demands that his audience subjectively interpret the values and qualities that provide salvation,
suggesting only that they are located within and not in
things.

The Tooth of Crime (1972) is Shepard's best rock
and roll play, incorporating music in a structural
unity that seems artificial in his other work. Shepard
has commented that "music speaks to everything at once,
especially the emotions," [15] and that "nothing communi-
cates emotion better than music, not even the greatest
play in the world." [16] His intent in this play is
clearly emotional rather than intellectual, and the
work demonstrates his use of both language and modern
myth to appeal to his audience on that level, culminating his experimentation with these techniques which
characterize most of his early drama. Tooth dramatizes
the conflict between an aging gunfighter cum rock-and-
roll star, Hoss, and his challenger, a similarly mythic
figure, Crow. This battle for supremacy takes place in
a surreal vision of the future in Hoss' fortress where
he is surrounded by his retinue of rock groupies,
henchmen, and astrologer. The duel is purely in terms
of style, reflected in their use of language, a shoot-
out of words. Hoss laments the challenge as the passing of a time when individual style was significant:

> Backed into a fucking box. I can't believe it. Things have changed that
> much. They don't even apprentice no more. Just mark for the big one.
> No respect no more. . . . Can't they see where they're goin'! Without a
> code it's just crime. No art involved. No technique, finesse. No sense
> of mastery. The touch is gone. (218)

The duel takes place, however, and Crow proves to be a
formidable opponent, winning by a TKO in the third
round, claiming Hoss' position as his prize, willing to
teach Hoss his style in return. But Hoss cannot learn,
for style is intensely individual and is inherent
within the character. He says, "It can't be taught or
copied or stolen or sold. It's mine. An original.
It's my life and my death in one clean shot" (251).
Hoss commits suicide, leaving in his place Crow, whose
name suggests the amoral, predatory, survival instinct
which informs Ted Hughes' poetry. Chief among the
points Shepard makes in this play is that people are

the manifestation of the manner in which they perceive
themselves, which in turn is also how they are perceived by others. Contemporary people create themselves as surely as they formulate a style to reflect
what they feel themselves to be. Through the use of
stylized, surreal metaphors, Shepard explores the
reality of artists swamped in the commercial side of
their art, implying his own position as dramatic
upstart. But rather than being about the idea of
self-worth and self-conception under the pressure of
success, it is a dramatization of that pressure. The
playwright demonstrates the process rather than the
impulse.

However, by the time of Geography of a Horse
Dreamer (1974), Shepard begins to examine the sources
of his characters' notions of self rather than simply
presenting them objectively. Clearly a metadrama
grounded in external reality, the play concerns the
artist of the imagination, Cody, a visionary held
captive to serve the materialistic ends of a corrupt
organization. Particularly problematic is the conclusion of this play; by relying on a deus ex machina
ending, Shepard weakens his metaphor of the primacy of
the individual perception of reality and obscures his
usual insistence on the need for internal harmony to
defeat the opposing forces of a materialistic and
commercial society that threatens destruction. After
this play, which is ultimately a dramatic failure, he
abandons his surreal, subjective mythic method and
adapts his experimental techniques to a more traditional realism.

Curse of the Starving Class (1977) is the first of
Shepard's family dramas and the first play by him to be
structured in terms of traditional realism, although
his variations on the form are significant and distinctive. He charts the final decay of a family who
live on a western avocado farm, examining the impulse
which creates the wanderer, the displaced individual
who populates his earlier plays, dramatizing the
corruption of values as they pass from one generation
to the next. As suggested by their names, Wesley and
Emma are simply variations, or variants, on their
parents, Weston and Ella. Although poor, the family is
in no danger of the starvation that the title suggests.
Significantly, a refrigerator, a machine, is the
central symbol in the play, and the characters are
never too far from it, rooting in it idly or going
through the motions of filling it to avoid the notion

of poverty and starvation, which in this work are spiritual and not physical. Hunger dominates the characters' actions and personalities: Ella's hunger for escape to Europe, abandoning the notion of family and the home which represents it; Emma's hunger to go to Mexico, also a rejection of both home and homeland, to live her image of a beat existence; Weston's and Wesley's similar familial starvation, their hunger to have roots and a sense of place; and Wesley's hunger to hold on to the farm, his past, present, and future--his heritage and sense of belonging and self-worth.

Weston is a more realistic incarnation of Shepard's displaced man; belonging nowhere, he goes on drunken binges and disappears for stretches of time. Ella and Emma are his typical women, whose existences are only tangential to the males and who seem to deny the bond represented by the family. But ultimately, the nature of the family as a representation of human bonding is the playwright's interest here, for even though these people are tied by blood, they are isolated from each other in their own perceptions of reality. They do not communicate, nor do they really attempt to; they are all locked into narcissistic conceptions of self and disagree about the literal and metaphoric nature of the home. The motif of a poisoned family runs throughout the play, in the form of being cursed by being "like liquid dynamite," which is "Something in the blood. Hereditary. Highly explosive" (152), to Weston's "outlook," which is "full of poison. Infected" (168), to Emma's first menstruation. Ella identifies the problem:

> It's a curse. I can feel it. It's invisible but it's there. It's always there. . . . It goes back and back to tiny little cells and genes. To atoms. To tiny little swimming things making up their minds without us. Plotting in the womb. Before that even. In the air. We're surrounded with it. It's bigger than government even. It goes forward too. We spread it. We pass it on. We inherit it and pass it down, and then pass it down again. It goes on and on like that without us. (174-75)

When Weston tries to stop this pattern of disease from repeating (a theme familiar from La Turista) to gain control of his own existence, he is defeated by forces larger than himself, and Wesley simply takes his place, symbolically donning his father's garments and following Weston's description of an epiphany. The environment and heredity win, for the play closes with Wesley having assumed his familial role, looking into the refrigerator for sustenance.

Four separate concepts of reality inhabit the same house in this play, and each has little to do with any other. In Shepardian fashion, Wesley early addresses himself and the reader in monologue, establishing his perception of reality and defining his consciousness (137); isolated and divided, each family member succumbs to the curse as he or she perceives it. Weston articulates the heart of the play when he states: "It was good to be connected by blood like that. That a family wasn't just a social thing. It was an animal thing. It was a reason of nature that we were all together under the same roof" (187). Shepard's use of the gangsters, Slater and Emerson, undercuts the failure of the family bond by introducing a deus ex machina disruptive force; again, resolution comes from without rather than from within. But despite this weakness, Marranca is correct in pointing to the significance of Curse because "it signals a landmark in Shepard's dramatic oeuvre, perhaps a turning away from an obsession with pop myth and counterculture themes to what is a more expansive world view."[17]

The promise signaled in his first dramatic treatment of the family in traditional realistic structure is realized in Buried Child (1978), for which Shepard won a Pulitzer Prize. Echoing Ghosts, The Homecoming, and The American Dream, Buried Child is "a three-act realistic drama for a post-absurdist age."[18] Set on a farm in Illinois, the situation and concerns are the same as in Curse, but with two dramatic variations: the presence of the outsider, Shelly, in a pivotal role, and the return of the prodigal son, Vince, from his wandering to embrace the past he had previously rejected. Again, the framework is recognizable, external reality, but the separate lives of the family members are closed and subjective, bound together only by the blood tie. In this play, Shepard probes one step deeper into the curse of the family, exploring and exposing the source of the poison.

Although all of Shepard's plays can be considered as extended poetic and symbolic metaphors, Buried Child is his first sustained work of conscious dramatic allusion. Constructed around the ordinary and the commonplace, the play is archetypal in its structure, embodying several layers of symbolic meaning, and functioning as a postmodern dramatization of The Wasteland. It opens with the quintessential American family in complete decay, a dying patriarch surrounded by wounded and maimed sons, an escapist maternal figure, and the return of a third-generation errant quester, a prodigal son returned to seek significance, meaning, and place in the roots he had once abandoned. On its most easily accessible and realistic level, it concerns the passing of a family farm, now barren, to a new generation, suggesting the possibility of rebirth and renewal. On its mythic level, the play dramatizes the inheritance of the sterility of one generation by a wounded but inward-looking postmodern generation, whose responsibility it is to unearth the past, purify it, and look toward the future.

Act I represents the past and outlines what has become of the family and farm that were once prosperous but have come squarely to face nothing but death and decay. The dying father, Dodge, the wounded fisher-king, recalls what once was:

> See, we were a well established family once. Well established. All the
> boys were grown. The farm was producing enough milk to fill Lake
> Michigan twice over. Me and Halie here were pointed toward what looked
> like the middle part of our life. Everything was settled with us. All
> we had to do was ride it out. Then Halie got pregnant again. Outa' the
> middle a' nowhere, she got pregnant. We weren't planning on havin' any
> more boys. We had enough boys already. In fact, we hadn't been sleeping
> in the same bed for about six years. (123)

As the play opens, however, none of the prosperity and security of this modern American dream have been realized by the family and the land it represents. Halie's pregnancy resulted in the "buried child" of the title, a new son, quite possibly the product of incest with her son Tilden (124). Drowned by Dodge in anger for its representation of perverted ideals and the convolution of the family line, the baby's body is buried behind the house and never discussed by family "pact" (123). Its corpse blights the land as surely as its memory blights the family.

The source of this curse is, not surprisingly in Shepard, the woman, Halie, who is clearly detached from the reality of the family as the play opens. Having long since escaped into her own separate reality of the past, represented by her upstairs room covered in photographs (86, 110-12), she is represented on stage only by her voice until the middle of the first act. When she appears, she is dressed completely in black, as if in mourning for the death of her family and her world. She speaks of the past before she appears, recalling having once gone to the races in Florida with "A wonderful man. A breeder" (65). Her recollection contrasts sharply with the reality around her; the unnamed man was, by implication, fertile in contrast to the dying and impotent Dodge, lying downstairs in the reality of the present, and she recalls the landscape as lush and blooming (66), the antithesis of the barren farm she seeks to escape by denying reality and seeking solace in a severely flawed Christianity, represented by the Reverend Dewis. Advising Dodge to take his pills for pain, she rambles more to herself than to the others:

> It's not Christian, but it works. It's not necessarily Christian, that is. We don't know. There's some things the ministers can't even answer. I, personally, can't see anything wrong with it. Pain is pain. Pure and simple. Suffering is a different matter. That's entirely different. A pill seems as good an answer as any. (65)

Answered by an assessment of "Catastrophic" to her question, "What's it like down there, Dodge?" (64), she begins the play in her other-worldly upstairs room, where she also ends it, venturing out only to spend the night with her flawed Christianity, her solution to "suffering," the minister who escorts her home on Monday morning, seeking only pleasure for himself, not spiritual or religious comfort for others.

Returning home dressed in yellow and carrying roses (113), Halie's casting off of mourning is false and superficial; the dress is only a temporary and cosmetic covering (she is untouched, for returning to her room, she again soliloquizes to no one in particular), and the roses (emblems of passion alien to the environment of this farm) are abandoned behind her in the reality of the downstairs. As the once-fertile woman, however, her early references to rain and vegetables introduce two of the dominant motifs of the play. Ambiguously, she heralds the rain that may or may not be falling as the play opens. Having announced the rain from the vantage point of her window in the unreal upper room, she says both "It's not raining" (74) and "Still raining" (77) before she leaves the house. As in Eliot's poem, the revivifying rain is suggested without being confirmed. Similarly, when Tilden appears with an armload of corn (68-69), both she and Dodge confirm that there has been no corn on the land since 1935. Breaking the objective reality of the play for subjective interpretations of reality, Shepard suggests

89

the promise of renewed fertility for this farm and
family without confirming it.

The symbol for this barrenness and approaching
death is Dodge, the rapidly expiring father. Confined
for the most part to his couch, he proclaims the
reality of the play catastrophic, and recognizing his
own impotence, tells his wife, "My appearance is out of
his domain! It's even out of mine! In fact, it's
disappeared! I'm an invisible man!" (68). Threatened
with symbolic castration by his wife and maimed sons,
the old man fears having his hair cut while he is
asleep (67). Once accomplished, at the opening of Act
II, he lies cut and bleeding, the wounded fisher-king
who tries to assert his authority feebly by snatching
his symbolic crown, a baseball cap, out of the hands of
the usurper, Shelly (86). The only character aware of
the impending extinction of the family, Dodge was the
only one to recognize the significance of the unwanted
child and the contagion it represented. He can admire
Shelly as a needed infusion of new blood in this
inverted family and outlines his priorities when he
tells her that she is "Full of faith. Hope. Faith and
hope. Yor're all alike you hopers. If it's not God
then it's a man. If it's not a man then it's a woman.
If it's not a woman then its [sic] the land or the
future of some kind. Some kind of future" (109).
Realizing that he is not the future, he rages in his
own frustration to effect any change in his family and
the land. To him the past is "A long line of corpses!
There's not a living soul behind me. Not a one. Who's
holding me in their memory? Who gives a damn about
bones in the ground?" (112). But in front of him lies
his grandson, Vince, the returning quester whose
mission has left him unfulfilled, who will come to
assume his grandfather's place and recognize his
ancestors, their significance to him, and his place
among them. After Dodge dies and the infecting body of
the buried child is removed from the land, both family
and farm can begin anew as a new generation atones for
the sins of the last two and looks toward the future
rather than being lost in the past or aimlessly drift-
ing in the present.

Although Halie believes that "It's kind of silly to
even think about youth" (118), she believes that the
third generation lies buried, literally in the yard and
metaphorically in the past. The sins of her generation
are represented in the dead child, whom Dodge murdered.
As he says, "We couldn't allow that to grow up right in

the middle of our lives. It made everything we'd
accomplished look like it was nothin'. Everything was
cancelled out by this one mistake. This one weakness"
(124). The other sons of the second generation are
hardly more alive. The one-legged Bradley is cruel and
self-serving; Tilden, home after his "little trouble
back in New Mexico" (70), is half-witted, but oracular,
a prophetic link between generations; and Ansel is
dead, a victim, in Halie's opinion, of Catholicism and
women (73-74). The promise he held dies with him, for
as Halie laments, "He would've took care of us, too.
He would've seen to it that we were repaid. He was
like that. He was a hero. Don't forget that. A
genuine hero. Brave. Strong. And very intelligent"
(73). As Act I closes, the full impotence and
sterility of the family (and land) has been established. The future holds no promise of rebirth and
renewal, and the last force of order and harmony,
Dodge, is symbolically buried by Tilden in corn husks
(81). But the corn has appeared, heralding a sudden
new fertility.

Vince, Tilden's forgotten son, is the "guardian
angel" of the family who returns from his quest unfulfilled, not to "watch over" (128) the family, but to
expose the contagion at its heart. He once escaped
from its closed system and followed his own subjective
vision; but finding that as illusory as the one from
which he fled, he returns after six years only to be
unrecognized: "How could they not recognize me! How
in the hell could they not recognize me! I'm their
son!" (97). As in Old Times, existence in the world of
this play is actualized through force of will; by the
assertion of self, self comes into being. As Shelly
says before her departure, and the climax of the play
(the first such in traditional form in Shepard), "Maybe
he's made this whole family thing up" (121). However,
Vince has only been forgotten as his dead brother/uncle
was forgotten, by family agreement. As he begins to
recognize his position, he tells his grandfather,
"Maybe I should come in there and usurp your territory!" (126), but force is not necessary. Realizing
the young man's abilities and significance, Dodge wills
the farm to him, appointing him his successor (129).

His companion, Shelly, finds the world of the
family and farm unreal, saying "It's like a Norman
Rockwell cover or something" (83). She, like the
reader, is an outsider, and the reader is invited to
view the world of the play through her eyes. In a

Pinteresque manner, the unnamed menace builds, and she becomes afraid: "I'm fuckin' terrified" (91). Recognizing her alienness, she asserts that "I'll do whatever I have to do to survive. Just to make it through this" (94). Accepting a passive role, she becomes the woman of the house in surrogate: she cuts and cleans the mysterious vegetables Tilden brings in, cares for the wounded Dodge, and sleeps in Halie's room. Symbolically raped by Bradley when he forces his fingers into her mouth (107), she has the temporary illusion of belonging, even to the point of seeing the house as her own (110), recalling Ruth in The Homecoming. But she cannot bear up under the pressure of the horrors buried in the family's past, and when Vince begins to assert his claim, she flees, underscoring the closed familial universe of the play.

The problem with the family that she can do nothing to help correct is its hidden secret, its dependence on itself to survive, its inbred dependency that has drained the individual members of the will to live, driven the youngest from the home, and now serves to bind them together in guilt. The symbol of this lack of vitality and inversion is the actual corpse of the buried child which must be resurrected from the barren land, and Vince is the force of vitality, a surrogate for his dead brother, the outsider who returns to revivify the land and renew the family, simultaneously a postmodern quester, seeking answers within himself and the family which represents his generation, and the fisher-king, ready to assume the crown of the fallen king. He has his own epiphany when he realizes his identity in his heritage. Seeing his own reflection in his car mirror as he tries to escape, he sees "another man. As though I could see his whole race behind him. . . . I saw him dead and alive at the same time. . . . His face became his father's face. . . . And his father's face changed to his Grandfather's face. And it went on like that. Changing. Clear back to faces I'd never seen before but still recognized" (130). A refutation of Dodge's line of corpses, this vision parallels Weston's realization in Curse of his own identity and is the only Shepardian aria in this play, for the isolation the characters live is not reflected in the structure, but suggested in their unfamilial treatment of each other. When Vince dismisses Shelly by saying "I've gotta carry on the line. I've gotta see to it that things keep rolling" (130), he recognizes not only his own identity, but transcends his savior role to become a symbol of any succeeding generation that must accept responsibility for the future. The wanderer must choose his home as Vince has, for he possesses none inherently, symbolized here by the family's refusal to recognize him. Vince's decision to stay is not based on direct family ties which are inescapable, but in his choice to assume the role. He recreates himself, as does Wesley in Curse, but by choosing to break rather than to repeat the pattern of his heritage.

As Dodge dies, leaving Vince the farm, and Vince takes his place as patriarch, literally and metaphorically as "His body is in the same relationship to Dodge's" (132), his father brings in the unearthed body of the child, and Halie's voice announces the coming of rain and the return of fertility to the barren land:

> Good hard rain. Takes everything straight down deep to the roots. The rest takes care of itself. You can't force a thing to grow. You can't interfere with it. It's all hidden. It's all unseen. You just gotta wait till it pops up out of the ground. Tiny little shoot. Tiny little white shoot. All hairy and fragile. Strong though. Strong enough to break the earth even. It's a miracle, Dodge. I've never seen a crop like this in my whole life. Maybe it's the sun. Maybe that's it. Maybe it's the sun. (132)

Although the rain may be simply another illusion from the upper floor, Halie speaks allegorically of Vince, the sun/son who, no longer hidden or buried in the past, has cleansed the land and promises the return to fertility. Archetypally, the questing knight reaches his chapel perilous, and braving the dangers, possesses the grail, revitalizing the land made barren by the wounding of the old king. Substituting the subjective myth of popular culture for literal and literary myth, Shepard achieves a level of allusion and evocative meaning untapped in his canon to date. The immediate metaphoric level of the play suggests the inward journey individuals must take into their own subjectivity, their own perceptions and memory, to uncover its hidden horrors and values, recreating self in a positive way and redefining personal reality in an existential consciousness.

Shepard's next play is a continuation of his exploration of levels of reality within the family structure; less mythic and more concerned with individual consciousness, True West (1980) examines the relationship between two brothers as they share a retreat at their absent mother's home in Southern California.

Set in a kitchen, the scene of so much of the new realism, Shepard demands that the play be presented realistically, for any other treatment would "only serve to confuse the evolution of the characters' situation, which is the most important focus of the play" (3-4). Within this framework of external reality, he introduces his two brothers who are polar opposites. Austin, the younger, is a portrait in middle-class respectability and a conventional achiever, while Lee is a Shepardian renegade, the displaced man who wanders about in the desert, living a fringe existence in crime and adhering to the anti-social, individualistic style of the hipster of the 1950s. The plot involves a deal for a movie screenplay about the "true" West which Austin is writing for a very commercial producer, Saul Kimmer. The conflict arises when Kimmer is more taken by Lee's inarticulate version of a story about the romance of the modern renegade cowboy, displacing Austin's concept. Representing the two halves of a single divided personality, the two brothers begin to drift from their seeming opposition to reach a common ground: Austin degenerates, doubting the authenticity of his chosen role, and Lee begins to elevate himself, rejecting his rootlessness for a newly found respectability. As Lee struggles to commit his ideas to paper, Austin begins to replace him in his previous role, stealing, drinking, and rejecting the family he has waiting for him. As William Kleb notes, "as the rational, self-controlled Austin crumbles, the realistic surface of the play itself seems to peel away, to disintegrate,"[19] and the reality of the play shifts from the external to the internal, a dramatization of psyche rather than event.

The script that each brother conceptualizes represents his views of self. While both ideas are romantic in impulse, Austin's is slick and commercial, while Lee's is rough-hewn and renegade. Neither conception of self, nor the sense of home both men reject, is viable; Austin emotionally asserts, "There's no such thing as the West anymore! It's a dead issue! It's dried up. . . ." (35), for the West, the uncharted space which was home to the rugged individual who pursues an individual perception of reality in isolation, does no longer exist, although both men desperately wish that it did. In an atmosphere laden with Pinteresque menace, threatened violence, and meaning expressed in a subtext beneath the half-articulated conversation, the brothers begin to merge into each other. Lee begins to want success and respectability

94

and Austin hungers for the isolation of the desert. They strike a bargain and a tentative peace: Austin will help Lee write if Lee will take Austin to the desert and teach him how to survive. But at that point, Mom returns, signalling just how deep into subjective reality the play has plunged. Obviously operating within the realm of her own perceptions, she is largely unconcerned about the decay and destruction she finds in her home and wants only to see Picasso at the museum, despite Austin's assertion that the artist is dead. No reality impinges on her consciousness. The two poles of personality collapse at this moment and the brothers, in a flush of animalistic territoriality, spring on each other. The play closes with them squared off, each waiting for the other to move, literalizing the sounds of the coyotes in the near distance. The potential ambiguity of the final tableau is in the nature of the self and the process of self-creation. Representing the Apollonian and Dionysian aspects of man's psyche, the brothers are too extreme in their stances to survive in isolation. Shepard dramatizes the collapse of such extremity as each half reaches out for aspects of its opposite.

On one level, the play is about artistic creation and is thus metadramatic; both men strive to create and realize their visions of the true West, as does Shepard. But more generally, it dramatizes the basic tensions inherent in any individual who tries to fix and define his or her own nature; imagination and actualization must co-exist, for neither is the path to reality in itself. Postmodern individuals are shown to be hopelessly divided, continually at war with conflicting images of self. As is characteristic of Shepard, the play presents a condition without philosophic argument; readers are given a case study, and it is up to them to diagnose individually the condition and prescribe for themselves.

With the exception of his recent Tongues and Savage/Love, written in collaboration with Joseph Chaikin, and revue sketches with primarily theatrical intent, Shepard seems to be moving in the direction of more traditional realism than in the beginnings of his dramatic career. The power of language and music, along with his use of subjective mythology, still informs his later work, but the plays are no longer dependent on these aspects alone for dramatic survival. Although still less concerned with structure and philosophy than impact and emotion, his reliance on a

broader literary and dramatic heritage which includes
and transcends his own subjective vision enriches the
evocative power of his work. Basically simple in
theme, the plays evince the postmodern technique of
dramatizing simultaneous levels of subjective, existential reality, providing his readers with a vision of
multiplicity and choice. By exploring the factors
which precede choice, Shepard effectively manages to
convey the subjectivity and isolation of the individual, the chaos and confusion from which any notion of
self emerges. His series of anti-rational images,
arranged episodically and bonded only by the process of
association characteristic of stream-of-consciousness
writing, dramatize the interiority of postmodern existence as the individual mind is dramatized apprehending
its own functions. Like all of the postmodern playwrights, Shepard indicates that displaced individuals
create themselves existentially, and any salvation to
be found in a fragmented and technological world is
within, not in the materialistic existence of things.
Reality, self, perception, and consciousness are all
subjective and interior; to achieve resolution, postmoderns must plunge inside themselves to find integration and harmony.

Notes

[1] Introduction, Sam Shepard: Seven Plays (New York: Bantam, 1981), p. xvi;
subsequent references to this edition and the plays it contains will appear as page
numbers in parentheses in the text.

[2] "Of Life Immense in Passion, Pulse, and Power: Sam Shepard and the American
Literary Tradition," in American Dreams: The Imagination of Sam Shepard, ed.
Bonnie Marranca (New York: Performing Arts Journal Publications, 1981), pp.
126-28.

[3] "Image Shots Are Blown: The Rock Plays," in American Dreams, p. 57.

[4] "Paired Existence Meets the Monster," in American Dreams, p. 111.

[5] "Men Without Women: The Shepard Landscape," in American Dreams, pp. 102-03.

[6] "The Tooth of Crime: Sam Shepard's Way with Music," Modern Drama, 24, No. 1
(March 1981), p. 18.

[7] "Visions of the End: The Early Plays," in American Dreams, p. 78.

[8] "Sam Shepard," in American Playwrights: A Critical Survey, ed. Bonnie
Marranca and Gautan Dasgupta (New York: Drama Book Specialists, 1981), I, 82.

[9] "The Genius of Sam Shepard," _New York,_ 24 Nov. 1980, p. 25.

[10] Quoted in _American Playwrights,_ p. 82.

[11] Sam Shepard, _Icarus's Mother,_ in _Five Plays_ (Indianapolis: Bobbs-Merrill, 1967), p. 55.

[12] Introduction, _Chicago,_ in _Five Plays,_ p. 2.

[13] _American Playwrights,_ p. 90.

[14] Sam Shepard, _Operation Sidewinder,_ in _Four Two-Act Plays_ (New York: Urizen, 1980), p. 193.

[15] "Language, Visualization and the Inner Library," in _American Dreams,_ p. 217.

[16] Quoted by Kenneth Chubb and the Editors of _Theatre Quarterly,_ "Metaphors, Mad Dogs and Old Time Cowboys: Interview with Sam Shepard," in _American Dreams,_ p. 201.

[17] _American Playwrights,_ p. 108.

[18] _American Playwrights,_ p. 108; John Simon, "Theater Chronicle: Kopit, Norman, and Shepard," _Hudson Review,_ 32 (1979, , 87, also notes the similarity to _The Homecoming._

[19] "Sam Shepard's _Inacoma_ at the Magic Theatre," _Theater,_ 9 (1977), 120.

SIX: PETER SHAFFER
Epic Psychoquester

Although with less subjective intensity, Peter
Shaffer's dramatic world is as deeply entrenched in
modern myth as is Shepard's. But the comparison
between the two playwrights collapses after this level,
for the two are antithetical in most of their techniques, demonstrating the diversity within postmodern
drama. While Shepard is intensely personal in his
vision and places style highest in his list of dramatic
priorities, Shaffer is more objective and very much
concerned with crafting his plays and their dramatic
structure. Both dramatists, like their contemporaries
and predecessors, are concerned with the interior
nature of the individual's perception of reality and
the basic divisions inherent in the postmodern sensibility and consciousness, but rather than devising an
entirely new means of dramatizing existential reality
as Shepard does, Shaffer adapts and refines the basic
tools of conventional realism. Just as Shepard represents a postmodern avatar of many avant garde experimental techniques which culminated in the late modern
absurdist movement, Shaffer stands as a representation
of the experimentalism that produced Brecht and Epic
Theater, less a development and extension of absurdism
than the probings of subjectivity evident in the works
of such a playwright as Tennessee Williams.

Shaffer has probably been the subject of more
critical ambiguity than any other major contemporary
playwright. On the most general level, his canon
defies facile categorization. His works, from his
appearance in 1958 with Five Finger Exercise to his
recent success with Amadeus in 1980, embrace a wide
range of themes and techniques and are not easily
labeled according to any of the major movements or
schools that have appeared in modern drama; they are
nonetheless distinctive. Informed as much by contemporary performance theory as dramatic theory, Shaffer's
dramas have inevitably achieved popular success, which

in itself seems to have inspired much of the current critical negativism. In an age that paradoxically exiles to obscurity its most acclaimed works, Shaffer has been able to entertain with theatricality while creating substantial dramatic literature. He eschews the metaphysical obscurity that has made much of Beckett, Pinter, and Albee difficult for a broadly based audience, without substituting platitudes for profundity, employing a presentation that is both experimental and engaging that avoids the esoteric subjectivity of Stoppard and Shepard. For his immediate accessibility he has had to bear the unwarranted attacks of being simplistic and facile, but his canon demonstrates that contemporary drama can be both entertaining and enlightening.

Even on his first appearance, Shaffer was not simply concerned with conventional naturalism, nor was he dealing with the polished surfaces of the playwrights of the 1930s and 1940s. His concerns were with the interior lives of his characters and he used the framework of the traditional domestic drama only as an objective touchstone. While much of Shaffer's technique in his structuring of his plays and his attention to external reality and character development are decidedly traditional, his treatment of his material and the issues he chooses to dramatize are distinctly postmodern, aligning him far more closely to the break in tradition represented in the Beckett canon than to the continuation of that tradition simply in a new guise. Like Shepard's protagonists, Shaffer's characters are individuals divided within themselves, lacking a firm sense of self, and representing modern questers in search of integration. The dramatization of the angst and despair of the contemporary, alienated individual, locked in subjective perceptions, is both Shaffer's subject and technique.

Unlike Pinteresque silences over an unspoken subtext or Shepardian pop speech, Shaffer's language is no more than that used by realistically conceived, articulate characters; his work is distinctive in structure rather than in surface stylization. Traditional, representational realism is only an objective framework for exploration in his work, for the reality of his drama lies in the individual psyches of his characters, not necessarily in their environments. While their environments may have contributed to their conditions, Shaffer is concerned with dramatizing that condition, not with cataloging the factors behind it. When his

100

plays open, his characters are seen at their moment of crisis, and it is their perceptions of reality and not the reality itself that concern him. Charles A. Pennel summarizes his usual pattern:

> He offers an apparently familiar scene or group of characters and arouses the expectations associated with them. Then, relentlessly, he strips away surface reality until characters and audience alike discover the true nature of the dramatic action in which we are involved. As we see through the conventional, we are forced to revalue past events in the light of our new understanding of the present.[1]

The true nature of Shaffer's reality is inevitably internal and subjective, and the framework of external reality, as in Pinter and Albee, serves as a gauge for the depth of his subjective explorations. Conventional realism is the most easily apprehendable level of his drama, and his work has been widely admired (and criticized) on this level alone; however, the true dramatic action in a Shaffer play is carried out on deeper levels, where subjective perceptions of reality come into conflict.

Therefore, Shaffer's affinities to the school of anger are no deeper than his adherence, on one level, to realistic social interaction by recognizable characters. His unique contribution to postmodern dramaturgy is the ability to apply the same technique to dramatizing subjective realities, and to this extent, he draws heavily on both Artaud and Brecht in their radically different theories. His most obvious attempt at Epic Theater is in The Royal Hunt of the Sun, a play also conceived and constructed on an epic scale. By dramatizing the clash of civilizations and philosophies in the conquest of Peru by Pizarro, he has the requisite epic historicality and sweep, and his use of Martin as a detached narrator is decidedly Brechtian. His use of Dysart in Equus and Salieri in Amadeus is similar in intent and effect. The three plays all have a stylized alienating effect, for while the illusion of immediate emotional identification is shattered, Shaffer betrays the essential epic impulse by creating an even greater emotional involvement by the intimacy of the narration. The reader becomes privy to the intimate workings of the characters' minds. The effect is intensely intellectual as well, for these narrators are the intellectuals of the paired characters in each play.

The subjects of these three plays are the minds and perceptions of Atahuallpa, Alan Strong, and Mozart; but

101

ultimately, these characters are inaccessible to the reader--each is locked into a highly individual and subjective set of perceptions: the views of the alien-god, the demented Dionysian, and the artistic genius. These perceptions, Shaffer seems to be saying, may be ultimately unknowable. However, he provides characters, Pizarro, Dysart, and Salieri, who perceive the others perceiving. These three figures are the access into the other three characters' minds. The reader is offered access into Atahuallpa, Alan, and Mozart through the minds of Pizarro, Dysart, and Salieri: primitivistic, ritualistic realities as perceived by rational, philosophic, and intellectual minds within the context of their own realities.

While this structure hardly reflects conventional realism, it is only tangentially epic in effect. A simultaneously detached and involved narrator ruminates on the nature of the character with whom he is paired (except in the case of Royal Hunt where Martin stands between the reader and Pizarro), forcing the reader into the same process of subjective consideration. But the process is intensely emotional as the reader is plunged into the narrator's own perceptions, thus belying the didactic purposes of Brecht's intent. By creating dual protagonists, Shaffer creates pluralistic dramas: they are at once concerned with the subjective perceptions of one set of characters and those characters as perceived by another set, whose probings constitute parallel but separate dramas in themselves.

In his attempts to create a "total theater," Shaffer closely approximates many of the theories of Artaud and his stated aim of creating a theater of "cruelty," the attempt to evoke strong feelings to affect a fundamental change in the life of the audience. By dramatizing the anguish of his tormented characters and making his reader privy to the assimilation of that anguish by his more intellectual narrators, Shaffer achieves just such an intensity of emotion. His utilization of the resources of the theater also conforms to Artaud's beliefs, and through stylized intensification of effects, underscores the emotionalism of his dramas. His most obvious use of these techniques is in Equus, which Helene L. Baldwin notes,

In terms of physical spectacle, sonorisation, involvement of the spectator, lighting, use of masks and of actor's bodies and voices, and in the lack of conventional realistic setting, Shaffer and Dexter [the

director I have approximated Artaud's specifications for theater of
cruelty as closely as it is possible to do and still have a viable
commercial success. It is true that in "A Note on the Book" Shaffer
states that Dexter's "founding fathers are Noh Drama and Berthold
Brecht," which may or may not be a disingenous leading astray.
Certainly, however, the total gestalt of Equus is quite different from
that of a Brecht play. Brecht is usually far more concerned with social
ideas than with purely personal psychological dilemmas.[2]

Clearly, Shaffer is not the disciple of Noh, Brecht, or
Artaud, but he does effectively apply selected techniques to his own vision and dramaturgy. The problem
remains, however, noted by Baldwin, that "all the
aspects in which Shaffer and Dexter appear to have
followed Artaud's lead are effects produced by the
director rather than by the playwright, a fact acknowl-
edged by the latter himself in 'A Note on the Book.'
. . ."[3] Collaboration notwithstanding, the stylized
minimalism and symbolic staging of Equus, as well as
Royal Hunt and Amadeus and the central staging inversion in Black Comedy, are aspects of each drama's
existence as a literary text and must be considered as
such. The stagings heighten the effect of interiority
and intensify the subjectivity of the plays and are
integral elements of the works, whether inspired by
established theory or experiments in immediate application of contemporary theory. No matter how these
effects came into being, they are integral aspects of
the plays as they exist within the realm of dramatic
literature.

Another Artaudian element of Shaffer's dramaturgy
and vision is his use of myth and ritual, wherein he
shows a close affinity to Shepard. Both playwrights
dramatize the postmodern individual's need for a system
of belief and both construct subjective mythologies as
alternatives to the contemporary spiritual wasteland.
As it appears in all his major works, ritual affirms
the necessity for subjectively apprehending and ordering one's individual existence in an inherently chaotic
world. He dramatizes a dialectic between a primitive
and an overly sophisticated character as they grapple
with the need for worship or attempt subjectively to
assign value in a leap of faith judgement. Primitive
man manifested his fear of catastrophe by deifying all
the sources for disaster, and similarly, Joan F. Dean
notes that such characters as Mark Askelon in Shrivings, Dysart, and Martin and Pizarro are all "closely
associated with the heart of a primitive culture is no
accident, for each recognizes that these civilizations

can fulfill spiritual needs in a way that Western culture and its Christianity cannot." She continues that "in both Royal Hunt of the Sun and Shrivings, as well as Equus, Christianity's inadequacy to channel man's need for belief and worship drives characters to embrace some ritualistic and primitive, if not home-made, religious system." She suggests that ultimately, Shaffer's "target is the basic structure of modern life and its diminished capacity to channel constructively man's spiritual impulses."[4] Like Stoppard, Shaffer seems to argue from an inherently Christian perspec-tive, but from his plays, nothing more specific than humanism can be seen as advocated; multiplicity is the postmodern condition. Like his contemporaries, Shaffer dramatizes people as alienated questers in search of meaning, of both self and existence, bombarded with their own sense of relativity in a world that seems meaningless. In Shaffer's vision, individuals must order the chaos by choosing to assign value subjec-tively, by choosing to worship, or believe, in some-thing which affirms their basic humanity and sense of community with others.

The immediate impulse behind most postmodern drama is the exploration of the multiplicity of choice, both an objective, dispassionate probing, as in Pinter, and the morally suggestive dramatization characteristic of Albee, Stoppard, and Shepard. In Shaffer, the same impulse is evident, but because of the tightly focused structure of his plays, choice inevitably hinges upon one major and specific issue. Shaffer does not combat existential fear as manifested in unknown menaces or as represented in the inanimate trappings of contemporary existence. His fear is the meaninglessness and futility of an undefined and uncommitted life, which bears striking resemblances to the concerns of his contemporaries while usually being manifested in the more conventional form of religion as a philosophical system for worship and belief. His major works are dramatizations of crises of faith, but seldom in conventional guise: the aestheticism of Shrivings and Amadeus, the brutal bestiality of Equus, and the sun worship of The Royal Hunt of the Sun are in no manner conventional to the Western mind and represent some of the alternatives the individual mind can apprehend and construct in a postmodern world wherein traditional systems of belief have decayed and collapsed. Conven-tional Christianity, humanism, and science all prove unsatisfactory as schools of belief in a relativistic age. While Shaffer does seem to advocate some form of belief, his objective stance to his material and his structuring of his plays around paired oppositions of characters underscore a multiplicity of choice and offer no easy solutions. The effect, like that of most contemporary drama, is to involve readers by forcing them into the position of moral arbiters between the oppositions.

Once one is in the objective realism of the play, relativity takes over and what appears to be realistic no longer is. Characters and readers alike are awash in subjectivity, for through his structure and staging, Shaffer's minimalistic sets become simultaneously one place and all places whose only objective reality is located in the individual mind. Similarly, the time continuum is broken as memory and subjective perceptions weave events into an impressionistic tapestry rather than a rationally chronological sequence. Both time and space are subjectively apprehended aspects of reality and are dramatized as such; they gain value and position only as the reader apprehends them, and such is the subtlety of Shaffer's skill that this aspect of his drama is seldom noted by those who attack him for his unfaithful representation of "fact." If Shepard's drama may be viewed as taking place on the pre-conscious level of the id, then Shaffer's work is intellectually placed two steps further, on the level of the clash of forces under the restraint of the superego.

Shaffer's first major dramatic effort, however, is his most restrained and traditional in form, if suggestive of the subjects that were to engage his further dramatic attention. Five Finger Exercise (1958) appeared in the first wave of the "new" dramatists, suggesting to critics that this new dramatic voice was less concerned with anger and the proletariat than with conventional drawing-room comedy of manners. As in Shepard's most recent work, Shaffer's subject is the family, the social unit that is supposed to bind and unite but fails, for each member is locked into a highly subjective perception of reality and set of values. While an "exercise" for the playwright in many ways, Dennis A. Klein points out that "Clive's recurring dream which Pamela relates to Walter is a metaphor for Shaffer's mode of writing the play: just as Mr. Harrington methodically strips the covers from his son, so the playwright strips the characters of their facades."[5] Shaffer is concerned with the isolation of individuals in their theoretically most intimate grouping and their basic inability to communicate. While not directly concerned with the nature of language (he seems to accept its inevitability as the only viable communicative medium), he does show an interest in the self-constructed illusions individuals create to protect themselves from any mutually agreed-upon notion of reality. In this play, despite its conventional structure, Shaffer demonstrates the same range of concerns Albee evinces in his more mature drama. The catalyst for the dissection of this family is Walter, their German tutor, the outsider who sparks each family member's reactions. Each perceives Walter differently, casting him in a role in an individual drama, and when he fails to perform as each expects, the entire facade of the family crumbles. While the family may be a microcosm of the decay of the Western family, the reader need not assume that the play achieves any more universality than is inherent in Shaffer's dramatization of the interior nature of any individual's perception of reality. However admirable a first effort Exercise may be, Shaffer has produced little in the same style, although it does stand as a highly promising, if misleading, beginning.

Shaffer's next dramatic appearance was with a pair of slight one act plays, The Private Ear and The Public Eye (1962), which expanded his experimental range and indicated that he was not to be easily categorized as a disciple of Coward, although both contain some of the elements that characterize his first play. The title of the first play signals its subject: the effects of idealization and romance and the resulting insular world constructed on private and subjective perceptions. Tchaik, or Bob, attempts to seduce Doreen but fails, and his brush with the grimy reality that his roommate Ted inhabits sends him back into his own subjective world, where he, like the hero of Britten's Peter Grimes, can live in isolation and dream of the ideal. The language of the play is reminiscent of Pinter, for social intercourse only serves to mask real communication and is ultimately flat and false. The Public Eye, however, is a more ambitious work. Thematically linked to its companion by being an exploration and character sketch of the effect of non-communication and isolation, its plot is suggestive of The School for Wives and Restoration comedy. Charles Sidley does not trust his much younger wife, Belinda, and so consults a private detective, Julian Cristoforou. Rich in the tradition of farce, the play examines how people create death-in-life situations by withdrawing inside themselves, using words as surrogates for existence.

Julian proves to be the catalyst the couple need, and through a series of machinations that owes much to the absurdist tradition, he offers them imagination and a sense of negative capability. He annonces the solution as: "End of words, start of action."[6]

Shaffer calls his next major work, The Royal Hunt of the Sun (1964), "an encounter between European hope and Indian hopelessness; between Indian faith and European faithlessness. I saw an active iron of Spain against the passive feathers of Peru: the conflict of two immense and joyless powers."[7] He continues that his "hope was always to realize on stage a kind of 'total' theatre, involving not only words but rites, mimes, masks and magics" (xii). It is epic in size and scope and has the Brechtian devices of a narrator and song; however, the effect is not alienation, but emotional identification. Artaud's influence is more evident, especially in the play's sheer theatricality, including dance, mime, and stylized stage movement, which result in a ritualized, musical effect that directly affects the emotions.

The play takes on large issues, as befits the epic impulse, and the roots of all of Shaffer's major concerns are evident here. Royal Hunt is intensely personal and is large in the same sense that the mind and concerns of Pizarro are large. He is an aging hero concerned with mortality, bitter and cynical, disillusioned with the human institutions represented by his entourage--chivalry, the Church, the king--as well as by idealized abstractions--immortality, honor, salvation--and material objects. He finds revitalization, if only briefly, in his encounter with Atahuallpa, the Sovereign Inca of Peru and incarnation of the sun, a human god. The Indian is the manifestation of what the Spaniard seeks, immortality which collapses time and forever preserves honor and glory. Pizarro says, "Everything we feel is made of Time. All the beauties of life are shaped by it. . . . I've been cheated from the moment I was born because there's death in everything" (64-65). His encounter with Atahuallpa meets this need for permanence and control, and he feels that perhaps gods can exist: "Gods on earth, creators of true peace? Think of it! Gods, free of time" (131). For Pizarro, this is the only way to gain significance: "It's the only way to give life meaning! To blast out time and live forever, us, in our own persons. This is the law: die in despair or be a God yourself!" (131).

107

However, Pizarro does not realize that the Incan's position is metaphoric of the existential capacity of all individuals to recreate themselves in any form they choose, investing self with a subjective set of values. Pizarro takes Atahuallpa's godhead literally and dies a defeated man when the Indian fails to revive after his execution. Shaffer's meaning, however, is clear enough: the natures of eternity, time, and divinity are subjective and relative to the individual. As Pizarro says, "What else is a God but what we know we can't do without?" (132), which in the play can be fame, honor, Christ, or the sun. Each man chooses to define himself in terms of that which he worships, thereby creating his own existential reality.

Like Travesties, this is a memory play, told by Old Martin as he recalls his own disillusionment about honor, which parallels Pizarro's. From Martin's small, personal loss to the destruction of a civilization, the play examines the failures of systems of belief; all the characters (except for the sacrificed Indian) come to see meaninglessness confront them, never realizing that the ability to infuse meaning lies in the individual's own power. The narrative framework of the play clearly indicates that it is subjective, a view of disillusion through disillusioned eyes. In his later work, Shaffer dispenses with this mechanical device, implanting both points of view within the structure of the drama, thereby creating one of his most significant contributions to postmodern dramatic technique, a duality of subjective perception.

In 1965, Shaffer produced another one-act play under pressure of deadline for Sir Laurence Olivier, directing the National Theatre, to be paired with Miss Julie. Black Comedy was later matched with The White Liars (1967), another slight play, for a New York production; together, they comprise "a complete evening's entertainment, on the theme of tricks."[8] While neither is particularly significant as dramatic literature, both are examples of Shaffer's attempts to expand his theatrical techniques. Black Comedy is a traditional drawing-room farce based on confusion and mistaken identity and relies on physical action rather than plot. By his inversion of lighting, Shaffer plays with the standard symbol of light as truth, ominously closing the play in the dark. The White Liars dramatizes the differences between givers and takers, implying that givers are equally selfish, for they can give a false role or fantasy. In the play, he examines the

private worlds of fabricated images of self, using a
tape recorder as representation of what Sophie thinks.
Ultimately, the innovations in both plays are amusing,
but dramatically clumsy, and Shaffer abandons them at
this point.

The Battle of Shrivings (1970) was rewritten by
Shaffer in 1971 as Shrivings and has yet to be produced
in this form. He calls it his "American play," [9] for in
it he attempts to dramatize "human improvability" in a
way he feels is indigenous to America, noting that
"English dramatic taste rather deplores the large
theme, largely broached: it tends to prefer--sometimes
with good sense, but often with a really dangerous fear
of grossness--the minute fragment, minutely observed"
(115). And as in Royal Hunt, Shaffer takes on the
institutions of a rapidly dehumanizing society, but in
a decidedly postmodern context, for as he notes, the
play reflects the social unrest of the Vietnam era with
its accompanying peace movements. Religion, politics,
and materialism are condemned by all four characters in
the play, so Shaffer provides little debate on the
nature of institutionalized beliefs, allowing all his
characters to denigrate them. The central conflict
here is the nature of mankind, whether it is improvable
or basically bestial and unredeemable through actions.
Represented in the conflict between the pacifistic
Gideon Petrie, a philosopher and president of the World
League of Peace, and the tormented Mark Askelon, a
poet, the play provides no answer, leaving the reader
to decide the significance of what has dramatically
transpired. The play ends with Mark beginning to
soften his almost primitivistic stance and with Gideon
breaking his vow of non-violence by striking his admir-
ing secretary, Lois Neal. Intellectual and dispassion-
ately dramatized, the play is an effective drama of
ideas, but because of its scope, it can be little more
than suggestive. Shaffer fails to provide any insight
into the subjective worlds of his characters, instead
preferring to remain entirely within the framework of
objective, shared reality. In both content and structure, this remains his most conventional play, repeating the pattern of the intruder on the familial situation, although in this case the family unit is founded
on choice rather than biology. Very much a play of the
late 1960s, Shrivings does little to advance Shaffer's
dramatic techniques although it evidences the same
concerns present in all his serious works.

The bulk of Shaffer's current reputation rests on

Equus (1973), which has generated a great deal of critical comment. As Baldwin suggests, "the play is controversial in its seeming anti-intellectualism, its implied criticism of psychiatry as a manipulative profession, and its apparent acceptance of sadism and bestiality as elements in religious worship."10 As in all of Shaffer's works, this play is not specifically about psychology or psychiatry, although the procedures and morality of science are called into question in much the same way as in Anthony Burgess' A Clockwork Orange; nor is it about sexual deviance. It is about worship and the need to believe in some ordering principle in existence and it dramatizes the possible perversions of this impulse in a postmodern society that denies individuals' Dionysian aspects in favor of their Apollonian sides. Two postmodern gods are clearly in opposition in the play: science and ritual, Martin Dysart and Alan Strang.

Dysart points out the true nature of Alan's problem, which, while created by his transferral of a basically sadistic Christian impulse to horses by the conflation of icons in his own mind, is rooted in a more disturbing manifestation:

He knows no physics or engineering to make the world real for him. No paintings to show him how others have enjoyed it. No music except television jingles. No history except tales from a desperate mother. No friends. Not one kid to give him a joke, or make him know himself more moderately. He's a modern citizen for whom society doesn't exist. He lives one hour every three weeks--howling in a mist. And after the service kneels to a slave who stands over him obliviously and unthrowably his master. With my body I thee worship! . . . Many men have less vital with their wives. (79)

Dysart's problem is not that he lacks the skill to cure Alan, but that he clearly recognizes the impulse from which the problem springs and its essential human vitality:

Without worship you shrink, it's as brutal as that . . . I shrank my own life. No one can do it for you. . . . I tell everyone Margaret's the puritan, I'm the pagan. Some pagan! . . . And while I sit there, baiting a poor unimaginative woman with the word [primitive], that freaky boy tries to conjure the reality! I sit looking at pages of centaurs trampling the soil of Argos--and outside my window he is trying to become one, in a Hampshire field! . . . I watch that woman knitting, night after night--a woman I haven't kissed in six years--and he stands in the dark for an hour, sucking the sweat off his God's hairy cheek! . . . Then in the morning, I put away my books on the cultural shelf, close up the

110

kodachrome snaps of Mount Olympus, touch my reproduction statue of
Dionysus for luck--and go off to hospital to treat him for insanity.
(81)

Alan has all the vitality, the capacity for worship,
that the postmodern man, Dysart, lacks. While the pole
Alan represents is extreme and impossible to live
successfully, Shaffer is suggesting that the norm that
Dysart represents may indeed be simply the other
unviable extreme. Dysart knows that "When Equus
leaves--if he leaves at all--it will be with your
intestines in his teeth" (105). He tells himself as
well as the boy that he can recreate him in his own
image:

> You won't gallop any more, Alan. Horses will be quite safe. You'll save
> your pennies every week, till you can change that scooter in for a car,
> and put the odd fifty P on the gee-gees, quite forgetting that they were
> ever anything more to you than bearers of little profits and little
> losses. You will, however, be without pain. More or less completely
> without pain. (106)

To save Alan the pain of his worship, he must reduce
him to the anesthetized state he himself is in.

Labeling Alan "a perfect anti-hero for the decade,"
Gene A. Plunka believes that "Equus speaks for an era;
it is the raison d'etre of a period in history in which
individuals are trying to find themselves by turning
away from social and political problems." [11] The world
and reality of the play are interior, and the reader
approaches a perception of Alan through Dysart's perceptions. The core reality of the play may lie in the
story told Shaffer on which he has based the play, but
in terms of the drama itself (which is ultimately
metadramatic), the objective reality lies in the environmental factors which lead to Alan's world of total
subjective perceptions. The plot of the work concerns
how he came to the hospital and how he is treated for
his disorder, but the subjective level of reality
behind the plot is the revelation of Alan's worship as
he perceives it. That level is in turn filtered
through Dysart's apprehension of it and his juxtaposition of Alan's subjective reality upon his own. The
reader is finally presented with these multilayered
realities primarily through Dysart's almost interior
monologues and the enactment of his exorcism of Equus
from the boy.

The play is structured to reflect these multiple

versions of the same reality. Readers are asked to believe they are in the doctor's office, the Strang home, the theater, or the stable, but one expressionistic setting serves for all places. In production, the audience, or at least a segment of it, is seated on stage, and the actors are always present, stepping into the playing area only if they are to function within the frame of objective reality, although they can speak from without (also the origin of the Equus noise which signals the presence of the god). The horses themselves are clearly human, their "horseness" only suggested in minimalistic costuming, representing man's inherent anthropomorphic instinct in assigning divinity. The entire mise en scène is constructed to represent a single mind in the process of apprehending its own workings, individually in the case of each character, but extending to include the audience as well, heralded by its presence on stage. Both time and space are broken as the play constructs itself in bits and pieces, jumping in place and shifting in time through flashback and reenactment. The entire construction of the play, from its impressionistic structure to its staging, suggests a representation of subjective, intensely personal perception, and thus is a dramatization of the functioning of the individual mind. Where his contemporaries have dramatized separate conceptions of reality functioning simultaneously, Shaffer has constructed a play that attempts to reflect how those realities are apprehended.

In Amadeus (1979), Shaffer again employs the same techniques for an examination of the nature of genius, using music as a symbol for the juxtaposition of subjective realities. Antonio Salieri brings about the destruction of Wolfgang Amadeus ("Gift of God") Mozart from jealousy, resenting the pact he made with God for success, realizing that Mozart is God's instrument while he is only an imperfect reflection of the talent the younger man possesses. Once having vowed to serve God for being granted success, Salieri vows to thwart God by destroying this rival, thus becoming an incarnation of evil. Salieri says, "You gave me the desire to serve You--which most men do not have--then saw to it the service was shameful to the ears of the server.... You put into me perception of the Incomparable--which most men never know!--then ensured that I would know myself forever mediocre." [12] He continues to chart his course, existentially denying divinity and assuming complete control over his own life: "They say God is not mocked. I tell You, Man is not mocked! . . . I am

112

not mocked! . . . They say the spirit bloweth where it listeth: I tell You NO! It must list to virtue or not blow at all!" (52). In his postmodern version of the Faust legend, Shaffer once again returns to historical material, examining systems of belief in a situation wherein cause and effect seem to have broken down in a society that assumes just such a system; Salieri's rage eminates from his sense of virtue wronged.

Mozart describes music as "how God hears the world. Millions of sounds ascending at once and mixing in His ear to become an unending music, unimaginable to us! . . . That's our job! That's our job, we composers: to combine the inner minds of him and him and him, and her and her—the thoughts of chambermaids and Court Composers—and turn the audience into God" (64). To Mozart, music is the collapse of time and space; as he says, "A dramatic poet would have to put all those thoughts down one after another to represent this second of time" (64), which is the structural problem Shaffer tries to avoid. The play begins in 1823 and shifts back to 1781-91 through Salieri's memory, collapsing all the events that transpired, impressionistically dramatized, into the last hours of his life. As in Travesties, action is memory, and like in Equus, the reader knows Mozart only as Salieri perceives him. The entire world of the drama, hinged upon external, historical reality, is within the mind of Salieri and is thus subjective; his perceptions are what are at issue in this play, for at this point, even Salieri does not know if he killed Mozart. Ultimately, the reader must assign responsibility and guilt in the absence of a god who rewards and punishes.

Shaffer's importance as a major postmodern dramatist lies more in his abilities as a structural craftsman than in his role as a thematic or philosophic innovator. Never having evidenced an impulse towards minimalism, as have Beckett, Pinter, and Albee, Shaffer looks back to the theories of Brecht and Artaud to give his plays wider scope and effect; his dramatic impulse is to include rather than to exclude. Unlike Stoppard and Shepard, he does not create a totally new dramatic form but chooses to refine traditional forms to serve the same purpose. As in Shepard's drama, Shaffer's plays structurally reflect contemporary performance theory, uniting the aspects of theater and drama in his work rather than polarizing them, as had been the tendency in late modern drama. His symbolic settings are among the most effective in postmodern drama and exist firmly within the literary realm of the text.

Dramatizing the essentially subjective and thus existential reality of human existence, his canon demonstrates the interior nature of the human condition and the relativity of all perceptions and values. By breaking dramatic time and space, his drama often unfolds on the plane of memory, and his divided heroes search for a sense of integration and meaning in a multiple world. In his major works, he deals with the Nietzschian division of the Dionysian and Apollonian impulses in man, casting each aspect in the form of separate characters who must be viewed together as halves of one personality. They meet only on the level of the religious impulse, for Shaffer advocates a subjectively imposed ordering on an existence that offers people multiple gods. He maintains that the need for worship is integral to self-fulfillment and that people must make leap of faith judgements, dissecting the old systems of belief whose efficacy have decayed, and reconstructing a personal system that answers to the needs of the unique individual. By remaining objective to the quests of his characters, he engages the reader in the same manner that character-izes all postmodern drama. The individual reader becomes an accomplice in the resolution of the drama and is forced into subjective evaluation, for no easy answers exist in Shaffer's distinctive world of ritualized existential myth.

Notes

[1] "The Plays of Peter Shaffer: Experiment in Convention," Kansas Quarterly, 3 (1971), 101.

[2] "Equus: Theater of Cruelty or Theater of Sensationalism?" West Virginia University Philological Papers, 25 (Feb. 1979), 120.

[3] Baldwin, p. 121.

[4] "Peter Shaffer's Recurrent Character Type," Modern Drama, 21 (1978), 298-99.

[5] Peter Shaffer (Boston: Twayne, 1979), p. 32.

[6] Peter Shaffer, The Public Eye (New York: Samuel French, 1962), p. 46.

[7] Peter Shaffer, The Royal Hunt of the Sun (New York: Ballantine, 1964), p. vii; subsequent references to this edition will appear as page numbers in paren-theses in the text.

[8] Peter Shaffer, _The White Liars and Black Comedy_ (New York: Samuel French, 1968), p. 3.

[9] Peter Shaffer, "A Note on the Play: 1974," in _Equus and Shrivings_ (New York: Atheneum, 1976), p. 113; subsequent references to the two plays in this edition will appear as page numbers in parentheses in the text.

[10] Baldwin, p. 118.

[11] "The Existential Ritual: Peter Shaffer's _Equus_," _Kansas Quarterly_, 12 (1980), 96, 95.

[12] Peter Shaffer, _Amadeus_ (New York: Harper & Row, 1981), p. 51; subsequent references to this edition will appear as page numbers in parentheses in the text.

SEVEN: DAVID RABE
Subjective Realist

Having achieved the most immediate popular success
among his contemporaries, David Rabe has produced fewer
plays to date, among them a Vietnam War trilogy, an
essentially feminist drama, and a reworking of The
Orestia. But despite a slender canon, he has achieved
an important position among postmodern playwrights.
Like Shepard, Rabe deals in situations that are uniquely American on their most general level, but also like
his fellow dramatist, his vision and thematic direction
are universal.

In scope and intent, Rabe's drama represents an
extension and refinement of the school of anger which
dominated the 1950s. But Rabe's work, while grounded
in traditional realism, transcends its boundaries,
drawing upon both absurdist and epic techniques.
Philosophically as well, his drama is quite different
from that produced two decades earlier. The Rabe hero
has transcended an individual sense of anger and recognizes the inevitability of the social problem; the
plays dramatize what happens when anger proves futile
and people are defeated by the problems their society
has created. Despite his characters' often valiant
struggles to infuse meaning into their existences, they
are doomed to failure, thus prompting some critics to
observe that Rabe's dramatic vision is essentially
pessimistic.

Although social criticism is inherent in each of
Rabe's plays, his concern is not immediately with those
social issues, but with how the individuals react to
the situations they find themselves caught up in.
Jerrold A. Phillips correctly points out the central
conflict in a Rabe play:

Although David Rabe's plays always picture such problems as racism,
pervasive violence, sexism, and the shallowness of middle-class values,
it would be wrong to characterize Rabe as primarily a writer of problem

117

plays. More Important to Rabe, it seems, is his vision of existential
nothingness as the core of all experience. Indeed, the plays can be seen
as structured around a character who is led slowly, inexorably, and
against his will to a recognition of this nothingness. [1]

His characters search for individual meaning in a
shallow and dehumanized world, finding that the only
values which are not relative are biological, and that
no existing system of belief functions for all people.
As Phillips observes, they come to understand that
"behind these biological realities there is nothing.
All meanings, all values are completely arbitrary and
fall away under intense scrutiny. There is simply a
great abyss, and those individuals who are unfortunate
enough to pursue this dark knowledge must learn the
meaninglessness of all life."[2] On the social level of
his plays, Rabe is saying, as Walter Kerr observes, "we
are all--black, white, straight, queer, parents, children, friends, foes, stable, unstable--living together
in the same 'house.' And we can't do it."[3] There is
no social problem in Rabe's drama because there is no
level of social communion; individuals are isolated in
their own consciousness and must come to terms with
their own sense of meaninglessness by subjective and
personal means.

Since randomness is one of his major concerns,
Rabe's dramatic vision is decidedly existential. Like
Albee, he dramatizes man's confrontation with the void,
but unlike his predecessor, Rabe offers no immediate
solutions, for individual salvation does not lie in
establishing a bond with another human being. Each
character functions on the level of individual perceptions of reality, which never impinge upon those of any
other character. As in virtually all postmodern drama,
each character is isolated within personal perceptions,
but in Rabe, there is no way out of that isolation. In
its largest thematic manifestation, this problem suggests its own philosophic statement. Like Shepard's,
Rabe's dramatic vision is apocalyptic, but rather than
suggesting a romantic vision of salvation, he cynically
charts the barrenness of a postmodern existential
wasteland. Both people and society are in a state of
fragmentation and decay, and his readers see the
dissolution of ordinary individuals as they give in to
meaninglessness and the void. In this sense, his plays
are contemporary moralities, allowing readers to measure their own descent in reference to those of Rabe's
lost protagonists.

Like Pinter, Rabe uses the empty social speech, generally of the basically inarticulate, to suggest both the hollowness of normal social intercourse and the lack of communicative power of language. Inarticulation also adds to the sense of an important and unspoken subtext, conveying a sense of menace, as his characters use language as a means of masking their true feelings and as a means of establishing control over others. But Rabe's use of language is in the postmodern tradition and he does little to advance its use as a dramatic tool; rather, his concern is with the structure of his plays and how they reflect the essential isolation of his characters.

Each of his plays is structured differently, but all adhere to a basic principle; each play suggests a framework of objective reality but dramatizes the individual perceptions of the characters on a subjective level. The "real" action takes place within the consciousness of the individual, and reality is surrealistically and expressionistically altered to reproduce dramatically the conflict of realities perceived by the individual characters. The Basic Training of Pavlo Hummel takes place in Pavlo's mind, even though several objective settings are suggested in juxtaposition in the play's minimalistic staging. Owing much to the absurdist tradition, Sticks and Bones has a setting that functions as a metaphor for American normalcy and is constructed expressionistically to suggest David's imposition of his sense of reality on that of his stereotyped family. Streamers is Rabe's most traditional play and firmly grounded in objective realism. Both In The Boom Boom Room and The Orphan are impressionistic plays which chart subjective perceptions, the former being located almost entirely in Chrissy's mind and the latter being a symbolic rendition of The Orestia. Thus, despite the range of technique, from the traditional realism of Streamers to the impressionism of Boom Boom Room, objective reality is always only a reference point for Rabe's actual explorations into individual consciousness.

Because the war trilogy forms the largest part of his dramatic canon, Rabe has been labeled as a war playwright. But since he writes basically after the fact, any social criticism of the Vietnam War, or war in general, is only tangential to his main interests. As Craig Werner observes, "Rabe uses 'the army' as a metaphor for the impersonal social system with no interest in individuals except as minor cogs in a large

oppressive machinery,"[4] in much the same way that
Pinter uses organized crime in The Dumb Waiter. The
Vietnam War is significant not as an object of protest,
but as a pivotal historical event that has helped shape
the postmodern sensibility. While grounded in a particular time period, Rabe's plays dramatize universal
human concerns; war is not his obsession, but the
brutality and violence of contemporary existence are.

Rabe's first play, The Basic Training of Pavlo
Hummel (1968), was written first in the trilogy but
chronologically can be placed between the other two,
for it concerns the actual experience of war, as
opposed to the preparation and aftermath dramatized in
the other works. Rabe early had to defend the nature
of his play:

> In my estimation, an "antiwar" play is one that expects, by the very
> fabric of its executed conception, to have political effect. I antic-
> ipated no such consequences from my plays, nor did I conceive them in the
> hope that they would have such consequences. I have written them to
> diagnose, as best I can, certain phenomena that went on in and around
> me. [5]

He says that he chose war because it is a "permanent
part" of "the eternal human pageant" (xxv), not because
war itself was his specific concern. While the play is
realistic in impulse, it is structured as a realistic
absurdity presented impressionistically, for in it the
external is only a projection of the internal. Rabe
notes that Pavlo's "perceptions define the world"
(110), an indication of the interior nature of the
play, wherein the action is internalized, manifested
dramatically as apprehended by the title character.
Breaking the time-space continuum, Rabe dramatizes
Pavlo's thoughts on three levels: in Pavlo himself by
his behavior and speech; in Ardell, a character whose
existence is a projection of Pavlo's mind; and in the
structure of the play, which is stylized and can be
seen to represent "an event occuring far within the
dying Pavlo's mind" (xxiv). The play moves from
Pavlo's death in a Vietnamese bar to his basic training
to his experience in Vietnam and back to his death,
with the circularity of the plot suggesting the inevitability of Pavlo's predicament.

The play charts Pavlo's initiation into a mechanized and brutal world, and his basic training is a
metaphor "meaning 'essential' training (and intended to
include more in this case than the training given by

the army)" (xiii). Rabe's intent is not to chart
Pavlo's decline, but to dramatize the factors which
precipitate it, otherwise the play would not begin with
his death. As Phillips observes, "Pavlo's search for
the stars leads him into the abyss,"[6] and this existential meaninglessness is what Rabe dramatizes, in much
the same way Albee does in A Delicate Balance, but
without Albee's suggestion of survival. Rabe observes
that "toughness and cynicism replace open eagerness,
but he will learn only that he is lost, not how, why,
or even where. His talent is for leaping into the
fire" (110).

In the limbo of the play's last few minutes (Ardell
tells the audience, "He don't die right off. Take him
four days, thirty-eight minutes. And he don't say
nothing to nobody in all that time" [106]), Pavlo
meditates on the nature of his experience in an imaginary dialogue with Ardell literally represented in the
text, concluding "It all shit!" (107). But Pavlo's
insight is too late and it offers him no promise of
salvation, only a vision of waste and futility. He
finds the "meaning" of his life, recognizing that the
social constructs in which he had placed his faith are
empty, and stares into the void of nothingness. The
play closes as the lights go out on Pavlo's interior
reality in death. The world no longer exists because
he no longer perceives it.

The second play of the trilogy, Sticks and Bones
(1968), falls third in the series chronologically, for
it concerns the return of the Vietnam veteran and the
reactions of his family. According to Rabe, it is
written in a "nonreal style" (xiv), which "lives in a
middle ground between what is thought of in theater
terms as 'realism' and 'fantasy'" (xxii). He also
notes that "the forms referred to during the time of
writing Sticks and Bones were farce, horror movie, TV
situation comedy" (226), which, like in Shepard, create
an immediate atmosphere of immersion in popular culture. On one level, the play is absurdist, for the
family Rabe dramatizes is very close in nature and
presentation to Albee's typical American group in The
American Dream. Their values, behavior, and language
are all stereotyped and cliché-ridden as the play
opens; they are all surface and live in a completely
superficial and trivial world. Their flatness is
suggested by their names, taken from the television
family comedy, The Adventures of Ozzie and Harriet,
although Rabe admits that "there was a time when the

121

names Andy, Ginger, Daniel, and Bucky seemed a more aesthetically appropriate choice . . ." (xxiv). But Rabe needs the immediate associations attached to these names, for once he has established the seeming absurdity of the world of the play, he immediately undercuts the audience's expectations by expanding the depth of the reality he dramatizes.

Language is central to Rabe's technique in shifting the mode of the play from absurdism to the level of existential reality. He comments that "one of the major conflicts between the characters in Sticks and Bones is a disagreement about the nature of the world in which they are living, or, in other words, about the kind of language that is used to define experience . . . . The simple, real event is hidden by each character in the language he uses" (xx). In this way, the dramatist attacks the family as a social unit that blocks rather than promotes communication, but this is tangential to his main purpose: to contrast this superficiality with the interior reality David brings into their home. This conflict divides both the family and the play into three levels: Harriet and Ricky cling more firmly to nonthinking superficiality in reaction to David's existential awareness of nothingness, catching Ozzie between the two poles and providing the dramatic conflict in the play.

Phillips notes that David's blindness is both literal and symbolic, for he "can no longer find any meaning in middle-class suburban existence"; therefore, "David's condition is fixed from the beginning of the play. What is of interest is the effect he has on the other members of the family." As a consequence, Ozzie "becomes the focus of the play. Whereas David represents an annoyance, an inconvenience, to Rick and Harriet, Ozzie begins to share David's perceptions, and gradually finds himself transformed from the pleasant, accepting, believing individual he was at the beginning of the play into the nihilist" who comes to question all the assumptions represented by the family structure.[7] While Harriet can ignore such questions as David's "Why didn't you tell me what I was?" (145) by ignoring them or by turning to the superficial family priest, Ozzie cannot. David says that he is "a young . . . blind man in a room . . . in a house in the dark, raising nothing in a gesture of no meaning toward two voices who are not speaking . . . of a certain . . . incredible . . . connection!" (162), and that "We make signs in the dark. You know yours. I understand my own. We share . . . coffee!" (163). In a manner highly reminiscent of Pinter, Rabe uses David as the intruder who threatens the security of the room by undermining the dishonesty of the family, forcing the other characters into a reassessment of their values. Zung accompanies him as a literal representation of what the family most fears, unseen by the others until Ozzie's final and brutal awakening to David's sense of subjective reality. As Rabe notes, the play is "as much about obsession as it is about tribalism--a more inclusive term than 'racism'--just as I consider the root of racism to be sex, or more exactly miscegenation" (xxiii). The girl represents the threat of the dissolution of the purity of the family, an expansion of its being, while the family fights for sterile enclosure and stasis.

David's perceptions soon begin to impinge on Ozzie's false sense of complacency, and the father begins to detach from the shared reality of the family under David's influence, plunging himself into a subjective reality that is new and frightening to him. Ozzie's first impulse is escape:

> I have this notion of wanting some . . . thing . . . some material thing, and I've built it. And then there's this feeling I'm of value, that I'm on my way--I mean, moving--and I'm going to come to something eventually, some kind of achievement. All these feelings of a child . . . in me. . . . They shoot through me and then they're gone and they're not anything . . . anymore. But it's . . . a . . . it sometimes . . . all brick and stone . . . coils of steel. (167)

While afraid of the change he feels coming, he is unable to wall himself off from his son's relentless judgements. David says, "I feel reverence for the air and the air is empty" (187), telling Ozzie that the material thing his father most highly prizes, the house, is "a coffin" (194). Ozzie continues to explore his own perceptions and delves deeper into his own subjective reality:

> I mean, I look for explanations. I look inside myself. For an explanation. I mean, I look inside my self. As I would look into water . . . or the sky . . . the ocean. They're silver. Answers . . . silver and elusive . . . like fish. But if you can catch them in the sea . . . hook them as they flash by, snatch them . . . drag them down like birds from the sky . . . against all their struggle . . . when you're adrift . . . and starving . . . they . . . can help you live. (173)

He tries to minimalize his problem, saying "I got a

minor problem of ambiguity goin' for me here, is all,
and you're exaggerating everything all out of propor-
tion" (197), but as David points out, "This is the way
you start, Dad. We'll be runners. Dad and Dave!"
(204). But there is nothing to run from or to, except
the awareness of nothingness. David says, "he doesn't
know how when you finally see yourself, there's nothing
really there to see . . ." (214). Eventually, Ozzie
cannot stand the pressure of seeing into himself, and
together with the family, he forces David into a
ritualistic suicide, purging the family of its disruptive element. Nothingness is ultimately inescapable,
and Ozzie knows this; he can only opt for what he
thinks is solipsistic ease, saying "of course, we die,
too. . . . Later on, I mean. And nothing stops it.
Not wars . . . or walls . . . or even guitars" (222).

In this cynical portrait of existential meaninglessness and the need for the confrontation with the
void, Rabe manipulates reality on multiple levels.
There is the absurdity of the cliché which masks
thought, represented by the family; the interior,
subjective reality of the nihilistic David; and the
pained self-explorations of Ozzie as he fights to avoid
the inevitable. All three levels of reality function
simultaneously in the play, embodied in the characters
and reflected in their language. Rabe comments that
"often a full, long speech is used in this play where
in another, more 'realistic' play there would be only a
silence during which something was communicated between
two people" (225). In this inversion of Pinter's
technique, Rabe translates the unspoken subtext into
words which are empty and can be as easily ignored as
misinterpreted. Language is an impossible means of
communication with self as well as with others.

Rabe's The Orphan (1973) is a reworking of The
Orestia and is an interesting, if atypical, experimentation in dramatic style. Fundamentally, it is a
dramatization of the theory of relativity, exploring
the dramatic possibilities of two events in different
places appearing simultaneously to one observer. In
his collapse of time, the murders of Iphegenia and
Agamemnon occur at the same time and are reflected in
the two Clytemnestras. In the play, Rabe conflates the
reign of Aegisthus with the Vietnam War, dramatizing
worship in the postmodern world as represented in the
Manson murders, wherein revelation comes through the
drug state. As in Equus, Rabe contrasts classical
ritual and the concept of the gods' will with human

124

passions and scientific theory. Rabe himself considers
this play an advance in his technique by his movement
"even further into fantasy and 'theatricality'" (xiv).

In a less formal exercise, Rabe produced the more
contemporary In The Boom Boom Room in the same year,
which further develops the problem of descent into self
explored in Sticks and Bones. He considers the play
the touchstone of his canon to date, one that examines
the dehumanization of the individual in a context
independent of the metaphor of the war. Essentially
feminist, it dramatizes the self-explorations of
Chrissy as she attempts to infuse her life with meaning. The minimalistic staging represents all the
playing areas in the work, and the scene shifts impressionistically only as Chrissy perceives place. The
entire play is internal, taking place on the level of
her consciousness and structured around her perceptions, lending a surreal quality to the action. As
Chrissy tries new people and new beliefs, she grows
wiser, but more disillusioned and bitter, finding
meaning in nothing. Her descent into the emptiness of
herself finally leads her to working as a topless
dancer in a bar, wearing only a mask to conceal what
she comes to recognize as self. Treated only physi-
cally, she finally surrenders to this estimation of her
worth, realizing her physical reality is the only one
she will ever be able to perceive.

Like all of Rabe's doomed protagonists, Chrissy
surrenders the quest for self in nihilistic defeat.
Janet Brown sees the play as a feminist statement:
"The total inflexibility and final triumph of the
unjust hierarchy in the play make Boom Boom Room a
deterministic dramatic statement. The play is a moving
but despairing portrayal of woman as object in a rigid,
patriarchial society." 8   But Chrissy's descent is not
limited to the female experience, for as Rabe has
shown, a confrontation with reality always means defeat
in the postmodern world, unless one constructs a subjective and personal reality.

Streamers (1976) chronologically falls first in the
trilogy, for it dramatizes the condition of a group of
men all awaiting shipment to Vietnam. On its surface,
it seems to be his most realistic play, but the nature
of reality is the dramatist's major concern here. The
ordered, traditional reality of the structure of the
play proves to be a false facade and functions only as
a metaphor for the imposed system of order and external

125

reality represented by the military life. Each character is ultimately shown to be living within the scope
of his own perceptions, in a separate, subjective
reality that has little to do with the level of reality
they all seem to share. What Rabe dramatizes in this
play is the conflict between subjective perceptions of
reality within the context of a recognizable objective
reality.

Mike Nichols, the original director of the play,
has observed that "if the engine of the play is fear--
if everyone is plunging toward earth, as maybe we all
are--then what every character in the play runs into is
the varied impulse to grab someone else in the short
time left, and the equally varied rules about how that
can or cannot be done. That's what ties it all
together." Rabe elaborates on this interpretation:
"I'd say the play also contains the danger of overesti-
mating what we share with one another, the danger that
if you don't have uniformity of feeling with someone,
then you have no connection with them. That forces
people into making dangerous demands"; he concludes
that it is "about people trying to recruit others into
their own reality." [9] The characters in the play share
the reality of military life as a form of order, and
all face the unknown, or chaos, in the form of the war,
but each makes the mistake of looking at others and
seeing himself, betraying the fact that each is
isolated in his own perception of the reality that only
seems to be shared.

The streamers of the title allude to parachutes
that fail to open, plunging the wearer to his destruction, and function to represent the failed realities of
each character as he faces destruction from independent
and personal causes. As a collective experience, the
play charts the descents of several characters, princi-
pally Martin, Richie, Carlyle, and Billy. But Cokes is
the central character in this play, for he originates
the concept of the streamers, and it is he who is left
at the end of the play, dying of leukemia and indiffer-
ent to his previous prejudices, facing meaninglessness
and oblivion and singing a nonsense version of his
streamers song which has now lost all its meaning. The
protagonist in this play, however, only serves as a
framework, for his descent is illuminated more by the
actions of the younger men who attempt to come to terms
with themselves as they all face the same fears in
different ways. With all the younger characters,
perceptions of self and reality finally come into

126

conflict in a scene of violence and frustration "as the spectator watches ordered reality dissolve before his eyes."[10] The characters who are not literally dead are depleated or anticipating death, for no communal, social world exists in this play; reality is relative to the perceiver, and they only share impending doom. The effect on the reader is similar to the effect of all of Rabe's drama. As Kerr states, "to the degree that we admire the play, to the degree that we believe in it, we despair."[11]

Of all the major postmodern playwrights, Rabe's thematic range is the most limited and his experimentation most narrow, at least to date. But this in no way reflects upon the accomplishments he has already achieved. His vision of the world as a postmodern existential desert and modern society as a shallow and dehumanizing force is representative of his era and philosophically aligned with the body of postmodern drama evolved from Beckett. His attention to the function and dramatic uses of language is clearly derived from Pinter, although Rabe often chooses to invert the system the Englishman most often employs. Like Albee, Rabe writes drama of social protest on one level, using institutions such as the family as objective reference points for his more subjective explorations. Along with Shepard, he is concerned with contemporary culture, refashioning the trappings of ordinary existence into powerful thematic statements about the physical objects of the world that the individual tends to take for granted. As in Stoppard, his plays are pyrotechnic in their multifaceted structure, and like Shaffer, he is a dedicated craftsman, always conscious of the combination of dramatic elements he employs. While more plays will undoubtedly follow, the range of achievement in those he has written firmly establishes him as a major postmodern dramatic voice.

The influence of absurdism and Epic Theater are evident in Rabe, although muted. He often employs the conventions of absurdism, but as in Sticks and Bones, he chooses to undercut the audience's expectations by expanding the range of the absurdist vision. His treatment of language is clearly in line with the experiments of Beckett, but perhaps most prominent is his treatment of situations that are in themselves inherently absurd. Like the late Beckett, Rabe presents an almost nihilistic perspective of contemporary existence. His social and political interests in his plays, while seldom central to his drama, are in

127

keeping with the didactic purposes of the epic impulse, although Rabe never preaches. In his use of expressionism and surrealism, his works achieve the episodic quality reminiscent of Epic Theater, while subverting its impulses by turning inward for exploration and achieving an immediate emotional impact on the reader. Ultimately, Rabe cannot be viewed as in any particular school of development, for the nature of his dramatic vision is intensely personal and finally self-referential. His progression represents a refinement of a set of basic concerns first proposed in The Basic Training of Pavlo Hummel.

As is characteristic of postmodern drama, Rabe's plays are structured in multiple layers of reality, dramatizing the conflict of subjective perceptions. This layered effect turns the reader's attention away from the exteriors to the internal world of the individual, where people live in isolation despite their elaborate social structures and life is dramatized on the level of existential reality, contingent on but independent of objective reality. What both character and reader find in this interior world may be unpleasant, but Rabe suggests that it is an inescapable fact of life. Any sense of externally imposed order is a facade in Rabe, who insists on the relativity of all values and systems. By implication, he seems to suggest that if human beings are destined for meaninglessness, an existential pose is all that can provide comfort in an awareness of nothingness. If reality is not external, then it must be internal. But Rabe's characters, like his readers, must individually apprehend this concept, for he provides no answers; he merely dramatizes the condition of those who fail to construct a subjective, existential reality.

Notes

1 "Descent Into the Abyss: The Plays of David Rabe," West Virginia University Philological Papers, 25 (Feb. 1979), 108.

2 Phillips, p. 117.

3 "David Rabe's 'House' Is Not a Home," New York Times, 2 May 1976, Sec. 2, p. 5.

4 "Primal Screams and Nonsense Rhymes: David Rabe's Revolt," Educational Theatre Journal, 30 (1978), 518.

[5] David Rabe, Introduction, _The Basic Training of Pavlo Hummel and Sticks and Bones_ (New York: Viking, 1973), p. xxv; subsequent references to this introduction and the two plays in this edition will appear as page numbers in parentheses in the text.

[6] Phillips, p. 108.

[7] Phillips, p. 111.

[8] _Feminist Drama: Definitions and Critical Analysis_ (Metuchen, NJ: Scarecrow, 1979), p. 54.

[9] Quoted in Robert Berkvist, "How Nichols and Rabe Shaped 'Streamers,'" _New York Times_, 25 April 1976, Sec. 2, p. 12.

[10] Phillips, p. 115.

[11] Kerr, p. 5.

EIGHT: A CONCLUSION
New Potential

Tom F. Driver argues that "the modern theater can best be interpreted as a paradigm of the development of modern consciousness in Europe and America." He continues to assert that,

In the postmodern period, man seems, for better or worse, and whether consciously or unconsciously, to be attempting to find some mode of self-understanding that is different from the histrionic, to see himself as something other than an actor upon a world stage, to see himself as oriented in a way other than in space, and to see the patterns of his life in something other than ritual form.[1]

It is specifically this problem which postmodern playwrights attempt to address, searching for new forms to reproduce aesthetically a distinctly postmodern sense of dislocation and isolation. To do this, they have chosen to adapt the tools which they inherited from the last of the moderns, modifying traditional surface realism, as Ruby Cohn maintains, "in the urgency of probing into deeper levels of reality."[2] Martin Esslin suggests that these postmoderns' "recognition of the subjective nature of all perception marks the really decisive breach with any theory of art that believed in the possibility of embodying absolutes, eternal verities, in enduring works. As such the naturalists were the first conscious existentialists in the realm of aesthetics." He also notes that "the need for form, new form, but form nonetheless, is greater than in the naturalistic theatre."[3]

In this exploration of the interior nature of the contemporary individual's existence, a variety of new forms have evolved, but all attempt to dramatize the nature of a subjective, existential reality. Also common to all postmodern drama is the effect this multiplicity has on the reader. The postmodern dramatic protagonist becomes "the spirit of denial, the man who says NO, pursuing his Yes down the countless

131

avenues of revolt,"[4] resulting in the fact that "the actions of each dramatic character (and, by extension, each human being) are explicable only in terms of that peculiar combination of forces, frustrations, and desires which is unique to himself."[5] Subjective in both form and content, this new aesthetic dramatizes the fact that "part of the ineluctable condition of being human is to live with the anxiety of knowing only penultimate realities";[6] therefore, as Esslin observes, "for good or ill, whether we like it or not, our Western society today lacks any . . . generally accepted system of ethics or philosophy. That is why contemporary drama merely raises questions, and refrains from providing solutions."[7] In form and concept then, "a play's meaning must include the meaning of our participation in its playing,"[8] and readers become accomplices in the world of the drama by providing their own subjective responses, measuring themselves against the subjective perceptions of the characters. The postmodern dramatist is concerned with action and choice, and the forces which precede choice, not with any absolutes which may be inferred from those actions. In a relativistic age, absolutes cannot exist, forcing the reader into a participatory role. Contemporary people have come to recognize that reality itself is necessarily subjective and therefore multiple, and that any verities that may exist are not to be found manifest in externals, but are located within, locked into the individual psyche. They have come to realize that shared reality is a myth and that individual reality is simply a matter of existential choice; this is the essential condition postmodern drama seeks to dramatize and explore.

Each dramatist has chosen his own means in his attempt to accurately represent existential reality, and each remains a unique and individual voice and vision in contemporary drama. Beckett, as a culmination of the modern tradition, represents the point of departure for contemporary playwrights. His expansion of reality inward in his insistence on the consciousness of the consciousness, wherein time and space are relative both philosophically and structurally, force the reader into subjective reaction and evaluation. In his circular, and thus inevitable, dramatic structures, he refines experimental techniques in an absurdist mode, providing many of the tools his successors were to adopt. As one of the first of the postmoderns, Pinter continues to attempt to define the limits of existential isolation, using language as reality and

action. Departing from Beckett's vision, he strives to
dramatize existential choice in situation rather than
in condition. Similarly, Albee's use of selective
reality achieves much the same effect, suggesting the
absolute necessity of constructing a subjective
reality, and he dramatizes the ascent from the void of
isolation and the power of redemptive emotion. With
their refusal to define human essence in minimalistic
drama, Pinter and Albee suggest the dramatic means for
the generation of playwrights who follow them. With
the rise of these two playwrights, British and American
drama achieves a unity of purpose unprecedented since
the dominance of the well-made play in both countries.
While both nationalities have begun to produce a body
of dramatic literature that evinces a native flavor, it
can no longer be viewed as nationalistic. Postmodern
drama is international in scope and concern, admitting
no particular national boundaries, and in Britain and
America where a basic realistic tradition has always
existed, the most significant efforts are being made.
With the infusion of Continental experimentalism to
this tradition, represented in the Beckett canon, a new
and unified dramatic theory emerges. Samuel J.
Bernstein argues that "the thorough bleakness to be
found in the Absurdist strain of the European writers
is diluted in the American works by a positive, affirm-
ative, high-spirited orientation."[9] This blending
produces a new dramatic aesthetic, one which refuses
the silence suggested by Beckett's development and
which, on the contrary, promises a rich maturity.

Each of these new voices is distinctive. Stoppard's drama evinces the postmodern obsession with
ideas, and his plays realistically reproduce the texture of existence in their blend of farce and philosophy, comedy and tragedy. In his celebration of possibility, he dramatizes the conflict of ideologies as
action. Shepard inverts this technique in attempting
the same ends. His virtually pre-conscious, pre-intellectual, and pre-literary plays dramatize an anti-
rational reality of rootlessness and isolation.
Shaffer turns his attentions toward the duality of
subjective perception and the multiple versions of
single realities in dramatizing the need for subjective
order, manifest in the need for worship and faith.
Rabe's vision is the most bleak in his insistence on
the absolute relativity of all realities except the
biological as he dramatizes social dehumanization. But
despite the range of techniques these four writers
employ, their goals are similar as they direct atten-

133

tion toward the interior quality of postmodern life. As John Killinger asserts, "our universe has imploded, and the drama that is vital and arresting in it now is psyche-drama."[10] Allardyce Nicoll maintains that "our age remains without a characteristic style of its own,"[11] but what exists is a plurality of superficial styles all employed toward the same end. Postmodern drama is unified in theory and aesthetics, which in turn are reflected in several individual styles. Form parallels content, for postmodern drama is most easily characterized in its insistence on subjectivity and multiplicity.

While postmodern drama is dominated by Anglo-American efforts, it is by no means confined only to these two countries; Fernando Arrabal and Peter Handke, among others, are clearly aligned with the same post-Beckettian experimentation. And the four major post-modern playwrights discussed here are simply the most distinctive voices of the new theories, not the only voices; both Simon Gray and David Mamet are clearly working in the same refinement of the tradition and many new plays appear continuously that evince the same aesthetic. By refusing to accept the cul-de-sac of absurdism without abandoning the techniques it developed, many young playwrights have grafted absurdist concepts to traditional realism, incorporating Epic Theater, performance theory, and the varied possibilities of theatricalism to produce a distinctly post-modern dramatic theory. The resulting new body of dramatic literature belies the late modern fear that drama was to lapse into silence, instead suggesting a rich potentiality.

Notes

[1] Romantic Quest and Modern Query (New York: Delacorte, 1970), pp. x, 469.

[2] Currents in Contemporary Drama (Bloomington: Indiana Univ. Press, 1969), p. 1.

[3] Reflections: Essays on Modern Theatre (Garden City, NY: Doubleday, 1969), pp. 18, 9.

[4] Robert Brustein, The Theatre of Revolt (Boston: Little, Brown, 1962), p. 16.

[5] Robert W. Corrigan, The Theatre in Search of a Fix (New York: Dell, 1974), p. 83.

[6] John Killinger, World in Collapse: The Vision of Absurd Drama (New York: Dell, 1971), p. 160.

[7] "Godot and His Children: The Theatre of Samuel Beckett and Harold Pinter," in Experimental Drama, ed. William A. Armstrong (London: G. Bell and Sons, 1963), pp. 144-45.

[8] Fields of Play in Modern Drama (Princeton: Princeton Univ. Press, 1977), p. 31.

[9] The Strands Entwined: A New Direction in American Drama (Boston: Northeastern Univ. Press, 1980), p. 7.

[10] Killinger, p. 5.

[11] The Theatre and Dramatic Theory (London: Harrap, 1962), p. 194.

BIBLIOGRAPHY
Selected References

General Studies

Abel, Lionel. Metatheatre: A New View of Dramatic Form. New York: Hill & Wang, 1963.

Armstrong, William A., ed. Experimental Drama. London: G. Bell and Sons, 1963.

Artaud, Antonin. The Theater and Its Double. Trans. Mary Caroline Richards. New York: Grove, 1958.

Atkinson, Justin Brooks, and Albert Hirschfeld. The Lively Years, 1920-1973. New York: Association Press, 1973.

Bentley, Eric. What Is Theatre? New York: Atheneum, 1968.

----------. In Search of Theatre. New York: Vintage, 1953.

----------. The Life of the Drama. New York: Atheneum, 1964.

----------. The Playwright as Thinker: A Study of Drama in Modern Times. New York: Reynal & Hitchcock, 1946.

----------. The Theatre of Commitment. New York: Atheneum, 1967.

----------. Theatre of War: Comments on 32 Occasions. London: Eyre Methuen, 1972.

Bigsby, C. W. E. Confrontation and Commitment: A Study of Contemporary American Drama 1959-1966. Columbia: Univ. of Missouri Press, 1968.

----------, ed. Contemporary English Drama. New York: Holmes & Meier, 1981.

Blau, Herbert. The Impossible Theater: A Manifesto. New York: Macmillan, 1964.

Bogard, Travis, and William I. Oliver, eds. Modern Drama: Essays in Criticism. New York: Oxford Univ. Press, 1965.

Brockett, Oscar Gross. Century of Innovation: A History of European and American Theatre and Drama since 1870. Englewood Cliffs, NJ: Prentice-Hall, 1973.

----------. Perspectives on Contemporary Theatre. Baton Rouge: Louisiana State Univ. Press, 1971.

Brook, Peter. The Empty Space. New York: Atheneum, 1968.

Brown, John Mason. "What's Right with the Theatre." Saturday Review, 11 May 1963, pp. 19-21.

Brown, John Russell, and Bernard Harris, eds. American Theatre. Stratford-Upon-Avon Studies, No. 10. New York: St. Martin's Press, 1967.

----------, and Bernard Harris, eds. Contemporary Theatre. Stratford-Upon-Avon Studies, No. 7. London: Edward Arnold, 1968.

----------, ed. Modern British Dramatists: A Collection of Critical Essays. Englewood Cliffs, NJ: Prentice-Hall, 1968.

Brustein, Robert. "The Crack in the Chimney: Reflections on Contemporary American Playwrighting." Theater, 9 (1978), 21-29.

----------. Critical Moments: Reflections on Theater & Society 1973-1979. New York: Random House, 1980.

----------. The Culture Watch: Essays on Theatre and Society 1969-1974. New York: Knopf, 1975.

----------. Seasons of Discontent: Dramatic Opinions 1959-1965. New York: Simon and Schuster, 1965.

----------. The Theatre of Revolt. Boston: Little, Brown, 1962.

----------. The Third Theatre. New York: Knopf, 1969.

Busi, Frederick. The Transformation of Godot. Lexington: Univ. Press of Kentucky, 1980.

Chiari, Joseph. Landmarks of Contemporary Drama. London: Herbert Jenkins, 1965.

Clancy, James H. "Beyond Despair: A New Drama of Ideas." Educational Theater Journal, 13 (Oct. 1961), 157-66.

Clark, Henry. European Theories of the Drama. New York: Crown, 1965.

Clurman, Harold. The Divine Pastime: Theatre Essays. New York: Macmillan, 1974.

----------. Lies Like Truth: Theatre Reviews and Essays. New York: Grove, 1958.

138

Clurman, Harold. The Naked Image: Observations on the Modern Theatre. New York: Macmillan, 1966.

Cohen, Sarah Blacker, ed. Comic Relief: Humor in Contemporary American Literature. Urbana: Univ. of Illinois Press, 1978.

Cohn, Ruby. "The Absurdly Absurd: Avatars of Godot." Comparative Literature Studies, 2 (1965), 233-40.

----------. Back to Beckett. Princeton: Princeton Univ. Press, 1973.

----------. Currents in Contemporary Drama. Bloomington: Indiana Univ. Press, 1969.

----------. Dialogue in American Drama. Bloomington: Indiana Univ. Press. 1971.

----------. Just Play: Beckett's Theater. Princeton: Princeton Univ. Press, 1980.

----------. New American Dramatists: 1960-1980. New York: Grove, 1982.

----------, ed. Samuel Beckett: A Collection of Criticism. New York: McGraw-Hill, 1975.

----------. Samuel Beckett: The Comic Gamut. New Brunswick, NJ: Rutgers Univ. Press, 1962.

Colby, Douglas. As the Curtain Rises. Cranbury, NJ: Associated University Presses, 1978.

Cole, Toby, ed. Playwrights on Playwriting: The Meaning and Making of Modern Drama from Ibsen to Ionesco. New York: Hill & Wang, 1960.

Corimer, Ramona, and Janis L. Pallister. Waiting for Death: The Philosophical Significance of Beckett's En attendant Godot. University: Univ. of Alabama Press, 1980.

Corrigan, Robert Willoughby. The Modern Theatre. New York: Macmillan, 1964.

----------. The Theatre in Search of a Fix. New York: Dell, 1974.

----------, ed. Theatre in the Twentieth Century. New York: Grove, 1963.

----------, ed. Tragedy: Vision and Form. San Francisco: Chandler, 1965.

Croyden, Margaret. Lunatics, Lovers and Poets: The Contemporary Experimental Theatre. New York: McGraw-Hill, 1974.

Doherty, Francis. Samuel Beckett. London: Hutchinson Univ. Library, 1971.

139

Downer, Alan S., ed. American Drama and Its Critics: A Collection of Critical Essays. Chicago: Univ. of Chicago Press, 1965.

----------, ed. The American Theater Today. New York: Basic Books, 1967.

----------. Fifty Years of American Drama 1900-1950. Chicago: Henry Regnery, 1951.

----------. Recent American Drama. Minneapolis: Univ. of Minnesota Press, 1961.

Driver, Tom F. Romantic Quest and Modern Query: A History of the Modern Theatre. New York: Delacorte, 1970.

Dukore, Bernard F., and Daniel C. Gerould, eds. Avant Garde Drama: A Casebook. New York: Thomas Y. Crowell, 1976.

----------, ed. Dramatic Theory and Criticism: Greeks to Grotowski. New York: Holt, Rinehart and Winston, 1974.

Elsom, John. Post-War British Theatre. London: Routledge & Kegan Paul, 1976.

Esslin, Martin, ed. The Encyclopedia of World Theater. Trans. Estella Schmid. New York: Charles Scribner's Sons, 1977.

----------. Meditations: Essays on Brecht, Beckett, and the Media. Baton Rouge: Louisiana State Univ. Press, 1980.

----------. "New Playwrights in America: An Outsider's View." Theater, 9 (1978), 38-40.

----------. Reflections: Essays on Modern Theatre. Garden City, NY: Doubleday, 1969.

----------, ed. Samuel Beckett: A Collection of Critical Essays. Englewood Cliffs, NJ: Prentice-Hall, 1965.

----------. The Theatre of the Absurd. Revised updated ed. Garden City, NY: Doubleday, 1973.

Fergusson, Francis. The Human Image in Dramatic Literature. New York: Double-day-Anchor, 1957.

----------. The Idea of a Theater, a Study of Ten Plays: The Drama in Changing Perspective. Princeton: Princeton Univ. Press, 1949.

Fletcher, John, and John Spurling. Beckett: A Study of His Plays. New York: Hill and Wang, 1972.

----------. Samuel Beckett's Art. London: Chatto & Windus, 1967.

Freedman, Morris, ed. Essays in the Modern Drama. Boston: D. C. Heath, 1964.

----------. The Moral Impulse: Modern Drama from Ibsen to the Present. Carbondale: Southern Illinois Univ. Press, 1967.

Frenz, Horst, ed. American Playwrights on Drama. New York: Hill & Wang, 1965.

Friedman, Marvin J., ed. Samuel Beckett Now: Critical Approaches to His Novels,
Poetry, and Plays. Chicago: Univ. of Chicago Press, 1975.

Gagey, Edmond M. Revolution in American Drama. New York: Columbia Univ. Press,
1947.

Ganz, Arthur F. Realms of Self: Variations on a Theme in Modern Drama. New York:
New York Univ. Press, 1980.

Gardner, R. H. The Splintered Stage: The Decline of the American Theater. New
York: Macmillan, 1965.

Gasciogne, Bamber. Twentieth Century Drama. London: Hutchinson Univ. Library,
1962.

Gaskell, Ronald. Drama and Reality: The European Theatre Since Ibsen. London:
Routledge & Kegan Paul, 1972.

Gassner, John. Directions in Modern Theatre and Drama. New York: Holt, Rinehart
and Winston, 1966.

----------. Dramatic Soundings: Evaluations and Retractions Culled from 30 Years
of Dramatic Criticism. New York: Crown, 1968.

----------. Form and Idea in Modern Theatre. New York: Dryden Press, 1956.

----------. Human Relations in the Theatre. New York: Anti-Defamation League of
B'nai B'rith, 1949.

----------. Theatre at the Crossroads. New York: Holt, Rinehart and Winston,
1960.

----------. The Theatre in Our Times: A Survey of the Men, Materials and Movements in the Modern Theatre. New York: Crown, 1954.

----------. The World of Contemporary Drama. Chicago: American Library Association, 1965.

Gilman, Richard. "The Absurd and the Foolish." Commonweal, 76, No. 2 (6 April
1962), pp. 40-41.

----------. The Making of Modern Drama. New York: Farrar, Straus and Giroux,
1974.

Gottfried, Martin. Opening Nights: Theater Criticism of the Sixties. New York: G. P. Putnam's Sons, 1969.

----------. A Theater Divided: The Postwar American Stage. Boston: Little, Brown, 1967.

Gould, Jean. Modern American Playwrights. New York: Dodd, Mead, 1966.

Grossvogel, David I. The Blasphemers: The Theatre of Brecht, Ionesco, Beckett, Genet. Ithaca: Cornell Univ. Press, 1962.

Hartnoll, Phyllis, ed. The Oxford Companion to the Theatre. 2nd ed. Oxford: Oxford Univ. Press, 1957.

Hayman, Ronald. British Theatre Since 1955: A Reassessment. Oxford: Oxford Univ. Press, 1979.

----------. The Set-up: An Anatomy of the English Theatre Today. London: Eyre Methuen, 1973.

----------. Theatre and Anti-Theatre: New Movements Since Beckett. New York: Oxford Univ. Press, 1979.

Helsa, David H. The Shape of Chaos: An Interpretation of the Art of Samuel Beckett. Minneapolis: Univ. of Minnesota Press, 1971.

Hewes, Henry. "Young Dramatists on Trial in the USA." World Theatre, 8, No. 3 (Autumn 1959), pp. 217-24.

Hinchliffe, Arnold P. The British Theatre, 1950-1970. Totowa, NJ: Rowman and Littlefield, 1974.

Houghton, Norris. The Exploding Stage: An Introduction to Twentieth Century Drama. New York: Weybright and Talley, 1971.

Hughes, Catherine. American Playwrights, 1945-1975. London: Pitman, 1976.

----------. Plays, Politics, and Polemics. New York: Drama Book Specialists, 1973.

Hunt, Hugh. The Live Theatre: An Introduction to the History and Practice of the Stage. London: Oxford Univ. Press, 1962.

Itzin, Catherine. Stages in the Revolution: Political Theatre in Britain Since 1968. London: Eyre Methuen, 1980.

Kauffmann, Stanley. Persons of the Drama: Theater Criticism and Comment. New York: Harper & Row, 1976.

142

Kennedy, Andrew K. Six Dramatists in Search of a Language: Studies in Dramatic Language. Cambridge: Cambridge Univ. Press, 1975.

Kenner, Hugh. A Reader's Guide to Samuel Beckett. New York: Farrar, Straus and Giroux, 1973.

----------. Samuel Beckett: A Critical Study. Berkeley: Univ. of California Press, 1968.

Kerensky, Oleg. The New British Drama: Fourteen Playwrights Since Osborne and Pinter. New York: Taplinger, 1977.

Kernan, Alvin B., ed. The Modern American Theater: A Collection of Critical Essays. Englewood Cliffs, NJ: Prentice-Hall, 1967.

Kerr, Walter. The Theater in Spite of Itself. New York: Simon and Schuster, 1963.

----------. Thirty Plays Hath November: Pain and Pleasure in the Contemporary Theatre. New York: Simon and Schuster, 1969.

Killinger, John. World in Collapse: The Vision of Absurd Drama. New York: Dell, 1971.

Kirby, E. T., ed. Total Theatre: A Critical Anthology. New York: E. P. Dutton, 1969.

Kirby, Michael. Futurist Performance. New York: E. P. Dutton, 1971.

Kitchin, Laurence. "Compressionism: The Drama of the Trapped." New Hungarian Quarterly, 18 (1965), 188-90.

----------. Drama in the Sixties. London: Faber and Faber, 1966.

----------. Mid-Century Drama. 2nd ed. London: Faber and Faber, 1962.

Kostelanetz, Richard. The Theatre of Mixed Means. New York: Dial, 1968.

Knowlson, James, and John Pilling. Frescoes of the Skull: The Later Prose and Drama of Samuel Beckett. New York: Grove, 1980.

Krutch, Joseph Wood. The American Drama Since 1918: An Informal History. New York: George Braziller, 1957.

----------. "Modernism" in Modern Drama. Ithaca: Cornell Univ. Press, 1953.

Lahr, John. Up Against the Fourth Wall: Essays on Modern Theater. New York: Grove, 1970.

Lewis, Allan. American Plays and Playwrights of the Contemporary Theater. New York: Crown, 1970.

----------. The Contemporary Theatre: The Significant Playwrights of Our Time. New York: Crown, 1971.

Little, Stuart W. Off-Broadway: The Prophetic Theater. New York: Coward, McCann & Geoghegun, 1972.

Lumley, Frederick. New Trends in 20th Century Drama. 4th ed. New York: Oxford Univ. Press, 1972.

Marowitz, Charles, Tom Milne, and Owen Hale, eds. The Encore Reader. London: Methuen, 1965.

----------. "New Wave in a Dead Sea." X, A Quarterly Review, 1, (1960), 270-77.

----------. "Notes on the Theater of Cruelty." The Drama Review, 11 (Winter 1966), 152-56.

----------, and Simon Trussler, eds. Theatre at Work: Playwrights and Productions in the Modern British Theatre. London: Methuen, 1967.

McCarthy, Mary. Mary McCarthy's Theatre Chronicles 1937-62. New York: Farrar, Straus, 1963.

McCrindle, Joseph F., ed. Behind the Scenes: Theater and Film Interviews from the Transatlantic Review. New York: Holt, Rinehart and Winston, 1971.

Melzer, Annabelle. Latest Rage the Big Drum: Dada and Surrealist Performance. Ann Arbor, MI: UMI Research Press, 1980.

Mercier, Vivian. Beckett/Beckett. New York: Oxford Univ. Press, 1977.

Miller, J. William. Modern Playwrights at Work. I. New York: French, 1968.

Moore, John R. "A Farewell to Something." Tulane Drama Review, 5, No. 1, (Sept. 1960), pp. 49-60.

Nelson, Robert J. Play Within a Play: The Dramatist's Conception of His Art: Shakespeare to Anouilh. New Haven: Yale Univ. Press, 1958.

Nicoll, Allardyce. The Theatre and Dramatic Theory. London: Harrap, 1962.

O'Casey, Sean. "The Bald Primaqueera." Atlantic Monthly, 216, No. 3 (Sept. 1965), pp. 69-74.

Oppenheimer, George, ed. The Passionate Playgoer: A Personal Scrapbook. New York: Viking, 1958.

Orenstein, Floria Feman. *The Theater of the Marvelous: Surrealism and the Contemporary Stage.* New York: New York Univ. Press. 1975.

Peacock, Ronald. *The Art of Drama.* London: Routledge & Kegan Paul, 1957.

----------. *The Poet in the Theatre.* New York: Harcourt, Brace, 1946.

Pilling, John. *Samuel Beckett.* London: Routledge & Kegan Paul, 1976.

Piscator, Erwin. *The Political Theatre.* New York: Avon, 1978.

Popkin, Henry, ed. *Modern British Drama.* New York: Grove, 1964.

Porter, Thomas E. *Myth and Modern American Drama.* Detroit: Wayne State Univ. Press, 1969.

Pound, Ezra, and Ernest Fenollosa, eds. *The Classic Noh Theatre of Japan.* 1917; rpt. New York: New Directions, 1959.

Price, Julia S. *The Off-Broadway Theatre.* Westport, CT: Greenwood Press, 1962.

Rice, Elmer L. *The Living Theatre.* New York: Harper & Brothers, 1959.

Robinson, Michael. *The Long Sonata of the Dead: A Study of Samuel Beckett.* New York: Grove, 1969.

Roose-Evans, James. *Experimental Theatre: From Stanislavsky to Today.* New York: Universe, 1970.

Rosenberg, Marvin. "A Metaphor for Dramatic Form," *The Journal of Aesthetics and Art Criticism,* 17, No. 2 (Dec. 1958), pp. 174-80.

Roy, Emil. *British Drama Since Shaw.* Carbondale: Southern Illinois Univ. Press, 1972.

Sainer, Arthur. *The Radical Theatre Notebook.* New York: Avon, 1975.

Salerno, Henry F., ed. "Focus on Popular Theatre in America." *Journal of Popular Culture,* 1 (n.d.), n.p.

Sarotte, Georges-Michel. *Like a Brother, Like a Lover: Male Homosexuality in the American Novel and Theater from Herman Melville to James Baldwin.* Trans. Richard Miller. Garden City, NY: Doubleday, 1978.

Scanlan, Tom. *Family, Drama, and American Dreams.* Westport, CT: Greenwood Press, 1978.

Schechner, Richard. *Environmental Theater.* New York: Hawthorne, 1973.

Schechner, Richard, and Mady Schuman, eds. Ritual, Play, and Performance: Readings in the Social Sciences/Theatre. New York: Seabury Press, 1976.

Schevill, James, ed. Breakout! In Search of New Theatrical Environments. Chicago: Swallow Press, 1973.

Schlueter, June. Metafictional Characters in Modern Drama. New York: Columbia Univ. Press, 1979.

Schroeder, R. J. The New Underground Theatre. London: Bantam, 1968.

Schwarz, Alfred. From Buchner to Beckett: Dramatic Theory and the Modes of Tragic Drama. Athens: Ohio Univ. Press, 1978.

Seltzer, Daniel, ed. The Modern Theatre: Readings and Documents. Boston: Little, Brown, 1967.

Sherrell, Richard E. The Human Image: Avant-Garde and Christian. Richmond: John Knox Press, 1969.

Sievers, W. David. Freud on Broadway: A History of Psychoanalysis and the American Drama. New York: Hermitage House, 1955.

Simon, John. Singularities: Essays on the Theater 1964-1973. New York: Random House, 1975.

----------. Uneasy Stages: A Chronicle of the New York Theater, 1963-1973. New York: Random House, 1975.

Smallwood, Clyde George. Elements of the Existentialist Philosophy in "The Theatre of the Absurd". Dubuque, IA: Wm. C. Brown, 1966.

Sokel, Walter H., ed. Anthology of German Expressionist Drama: A Prelude to the Absurd. Garden City, NJ: Doubleday, 1963.

States, Bert O. "The Case for Plot in Modern Drama." Hudson Review, 20 (Spring 1967), 49-61.

----------. Irony and Drama: A Poetics. Ithaca: Cornell Univ. Press, 1971.

----------. The Shape of Paradox: An Essay on Waiting for Godot. Berkeley: Univ. of California Press, 1978.

Styan, J. L. The Dark Comedy: The Development of Modern Comic Tragedy. Cambridge: Cambridge Univ. Press, 1968.

----------. Modern Drama in Theory and Practice. 3 vols. Cambridge: Cambridge Univ. Press, 1981.

Taubman, Howard. The Making of the American Theater. New York: Coward-McCann, 1967.

Taylor, John Russell. Anger and After: A Guide to the New British Drama. 2nd ed. London: Methuen, 1969.

----------. The Second Wave: British Drama of the Sixties. London: Methuen, 1971.

Taylor, William E., ed. Modern American Drama: Essays in Criticism. Deland, FL: Everett/Edwards, 1968.

Trilling, Ossia. "The Young British Dramatists." Modern Drama, 3 (1960), 168-77.

Tynan, Kenneth. Curtains: Selections from the Drama Criticism and Related Writings. London: Longmans, 1961.

----------. Tynan Right and Left. New York: Atheneum, 1967.

Valency, Maurice. The End of the World: An Introduction to Contemporary Drama. New York: Oxford Univ. Press, 1980.

von Szeliski, John. Tragedy and Fear: Why Modern Tragic Drama Fails. Chapel Hill: Univ. of North Carolina Press, 1971.

Vos, Melvin. The Great Pendulum of Becoming: Images in Modern Drama. Grand Rapids, MI: Christian Univ. Press, 1980.

Wager, Walter, ed. The Playwrights Speak. New York: Delacorte Press, 1967.

Weals, Gerald. American Drama Since World War II. New York: Harcourt, Brace and World, 1962.

----------. "American Theater Watch, 1977-78." Georgia Review, 32 (1978), 515-27.

----------. The Jumping-off Place: American Drama in the 1960's. Toronto: Macmillan, 1969.

----------. Religion in Modern English Drama. Philadelphia: Univ. of Pennsylvania Press, 1961.

Webb, Eugene. The Plays of Samuel Beckett. Seattle: Univ. of Washington Press, 1972.

Wellwarth, George. The Theater of Protest and Paradox: Developments in the Avant-Garde Drama. New York: New York Univ. Press, 1964.

Weisbacher, Richard Charles. "Four Projections of Absurd Existence in the Modern Theatre." Diss. Ohio State Univ., 1964.

Weisbacher, Richard Charles, ed. The Obie Winners: The Best of Off-Broadway.
Garden City, NY: Doubleday, 1980.

Whitaker, Thomas R. Fields of Play in Modern Drama. Princeton, NJ: Princeton
Univ. Press, 1977.

Wiles, Timothy J. The Theater Event: Modern Theories of Performance. Chicago:
Univ. of Chicago Press, 1980.

Williams, Raymond. Drama From Ibsen to Brecht. New York: Oxford Univ. Press,
1969.

----------. Modern Tragedy. Stanford: Stanford Univ. Press, 1966.

Wickham, Glynne. "The British Theatre: 1949-79." Contemporary Review, 236,
(1980), 89-94.

Worth, Katherine J. Revolutions in Modern English Drama. London: G. Bell & Sons,
1972.

Zinder, David G. The Surrealist Connection: An Approach to a Surrealist Aesthetic
of Theatre. Ann Arbor, MI: UMI Research Press, 1980.

Harold Pinter

Almansi, Guido, and Simon Henderson. Harold Pinter. London: Methuen, 1983.

Anderson, Michael. Anger and Detachment: A Study of Arden, Osborne and Pinter.
London: Pitman, 1976.

Ashworth, Arthur. "New Theatre: Ionesco, Beckett, Pinter." Southerly, 22, No. 3
(1962), pp. 145-52.

Baker, William, and Stephen Ely Tabachnick. Harold Pinter. New York: Barnes &
Noble, 1973.

Benstock, Shari. "Harold Pinter: Where the Road Ends." Modern British Literature, 2 (1977), 160-68.

Branmuller, A. R. "A World of Words in Pinter's Old Times." Modern Language
Quarterly, 40 (1979), 53-74.

Burkman, Katherine H. The Dramatic World of Harold Pinter: Its Basis in Ritual.
Columbus: Ohio State Univ. Press.

----------. "Earth & Water: The Question of Renewal in Harold Pinter's Old Times
and No Man's Land." West Virginia University Philological Papers, 25 (Feb.
1979), 101-07.

Davies, Russell. "Pinter Land." New York Review of Books, 25 Jan. 1979, pp. 22-24.

Dukore, Bernard F. Harold Pinter. New York: Grove, 1982.

----------. Where Laughter Stops: Pinter's Tragicomedy. Columbia: Univ. of Missouri Press, 1976.

Esslin, Martin. Pinter: A Study of His Plays. New York: Norton, 1976.

Fletcher, John. "'A Psychology Based on Antagonism': Ionesco, Pinter, Albee, and Others." In Rosette C. Lamont and Marvin J. Friedman, eds. The Two Faces of Ionesco. Troy, NY: Whitston, 1978, pp. 175-95.

Gabbard, Lucina Paquet. The Dream Structure of Pinter's Plays: A Psychoanalytic Approach. Rutherford: Fairleigh Dickinson Univ. Press, 1976.

Gale, Steven H. Butter's Going Up: A Critical Analysis of Harold Pinter's Work. Durham: Duke Univ. Press, 1977.

----------. "Harold Pinter: A Modern Dramatist." Science/Technology & Humanities, 2 (1979), 73-81.

----------. Harold Pinter: An Annotated Bibliography. Boston: Hall, 1978.

----------. "The Variable Nature of Reality: Harold Pinter's Plays in the 1970s." Kansas Quarterly, 12, No. 4 (1980), pp. 17-24.

----------. "The Writing of Harold Pinter: An Overview." The Literary Half-Yearly, 20, No. 2 (July 1979), pp. 79-89.

Ganz, Arthur F., ed. Pinter: A Collection of Critical Essays. Englewood Cliffs, NJ: Prentice-Hall, 1972.

Gordon, Lois G. Strategems to Cover Nakedness: The Dramas of Harold Pinter. Columbia: Univ. of Missouri Press, 1969.

Hammond, Geraldine. "Something for the 'Nothings' of Beckett and Pinter." CEA Critic, 39, (1977), 40-47.

Hayman, Ronald. Harold Pinter. New York: Ungar, 1973.

Hinchliffe, Arnold P. Harold Pinter. New York: Twayne, 1967.

Hollis, James R. Harold Pinter: The Poetics of Silence. Carbondale: Southern Illinois Univ. Press, 1970.

Kerr, Walter. Harold Pinter. New York: Columbia Univ. Press, 1967.

King, Noel. "Pinter's Progress." Modern Drama, 23 (1980), 246-57.

Kreps, Barbara. "Time and Harold Pinter's Possible Realities: Art as Life, and Vice Versa." Modern Drama, 22 (1979), 47-60.

Lahr, John, ed. A Casebook on Harold Pinter's The Homecoming. New York: Grove, 1971.

Martineau, Stephen. "Pinter's Old Times: The Memory Game." Modern Drama, 16 (1973), 287-97.

Morrisin, Kristin. "Pinter, Albee, and 'The Maiden in the Shark Pond.'" American Imago, 35 (1978), 259-74.

Pinter, Harold. Complete Works. 4 Vols. New York: Grove, 1976-81.

----------. The Hothouse. New York: Grove, 1980.

Quigley, Austin E. The Pinter Problem. Princeton, NJ: Princeton Univ. Press, 1975.

Schroll, Herman T. Harold Pinter: A Study of His Reputation 1958-1969, and a Checklist. Metuchen, NJ: Scarecrow, 1971.

Sykes, Arlene. Harold Pinter. New York: Humanities Press, 1970.

Taylor, John Russell. Harold Pinter. London: Longmans, Green, 1969.

Thomson, Peter. "Harold Pinter: A Retrospect." Critical Quarterly, 20, No. 4 (1978), pp. 21-28.

Trussler, Simon. The Plays of Harold Pinter: An Assessment. London: Gollancy, 1973.

Edward Albee

Albee, Edward. The Lady from Dubuque: A Play. New York: Atheneum, 1980.

----------. The Plays. 4 vols. New York: Coward, McCann & Geoghegan, 1981-82.

----------. Who's Afraid of Virginia Woolf? New York: Pocket-Simon & Schuster, 1964.

Amacher, Richard E. Edward Albee. New York: Twayne, 1969.

Bigsby, C. W. E., ed. Edward Albee. Englewood Cliffs, NJ: Prentice-Hall, 1975.

Cohn, Ruby. Edward Albee. Minnespolis: Univ. of Minnesota Press, 1969.

Debusscher, Gilbert. Edward Albee: Tradition and Renewal. Trans. Anne D. Williams. Brussels: American Studies Center, 1967.

150

De La Fuente, Patricia, ed. Planned Wilderness: Interview, Essays, and Bibliography. Edenburg, TX: Pan American Univ., 1980.

Green, Charles Lee. Edward Albee: An Annotated Bibliography 1968-1977. New York: AMS, 1980.

Hirsch, Foster. Who's Afraid of Edward Albee? Berkeley: Creative Arts, 1978.

Inge, M. Thomas. "Edward Albee's Love Story of the Age of the Absurd." Notes on Contemporary Literature, 8 (1978), 4-9.

Mayberry, Robert. "A Theatre of Discord: Some Plays of Beckett, Albee and Pinter." Kansas Quarterly, 12 (1980), 7-16.

Paolucci, Anne. From Tension to Tonic: The Plays of Edward Albee. Carbondale: Southern Illinois Univ. Press, 1972.

Porter, M. Gilbert. "Toby's Last Stand: The Evanescence of Commitment in A Delicate Balance." Theatre Journal, 31 (1979), 398-408.

Richards, David. "Edward Albee: Who's Afraid of the Critics?" Clarion-Ledger [Jackson, MS], 18 Feb. 1982, Sec. C, p. 8.

Rule, Margaret. "An Edward Albee Bibliography." Twentieth-Century Literature, 14 (April 1968), 35-45.

Rutenberg, Michael E. Edward Albee: Playwright In Protest. New York: DBS Publications, 1969.

Stenz, Anita Maria. Edward Albee: The Poet of Loss. The Hague: Mouton, 1978.

Vos, Melvin. Eugene Ionesco and Edward Albee: A Critical Essay. William B. Eerdmans, 1968.

Tom Stoppard

Babula, William. "The Play-Life Metaphor in Shakespeare and Stoppard." Modern Drama, 15 (1972), 279-81.

Bally, John A. "Jumpers by Tom Stoppard: The Ironist as Theistic Apologist." Michigan Academician, 11 (1979), 237-50.

Bennett, Jonathan. "Philosophy and Mr. Stoppard." Philosophy, 50 (1975), 5-18.

Bigsby, C. W. E. Tom Stoppard. Harlow, England: Longman, 1976.

Billman, Carol. "The Art of History in Tom Stoppard's Travesties." Kansas Quarterly, 12 (1980), 47-52.

Cahn, Victor L. Beyond Absurdity: The Plays of Tom Stoppard. Rutherford:
Fairleigh Dickinson Univ. Press, 1979.

Callen, Anthony. "Stoppard's Godot." New Theater Magazine, 10, No. 1 (Winter
1969), pp. 22-30.

Cameroux, David. "Tom Stoppard: The Last of the Metaphysical Egocentrics."
Caliban, 15 (1978), 79-94.

Cooke, John William. "The Optical Allusion: Perception and Form in Stoppard's
Travesties." Modern Drama, 24, No. 4 (Dec. 1981), pp. 525-39.

Crump, G. B. "The Universe as Murder Mystery: Tom Stoppard's Jumpers."
Contemporary Literature, 20 (1979), 354-68.

Davidson, Mary R. "Historical Homonyms: A New Way of Naming in Tom Stoppard's
Jumpers." Modern Drama, 22 (1979), 305-13.

Dean, Joan FitzPatrick. Tom Stoppard: Comedy as Moral Matrix. Columbia: Univ.
of Missouri Press, 1981.

Durham, Weldon B. "Symbolic Action in Tom Stoppard's Jumpers." Theatre Journal,
32 (1980), 169-79.

Ellman, Richard. "The Zealots of Zurich." Times Literary Supplement, 12 July
1974, p. 744.

Farish, Gillian. "Into the Looking-Glass Bowl: An Instant of Grateful Terror."
University of Windsor Review, 10, No. 2 (1975), pp. 14-29.

Gabbard, Lucina Paquet. "Stoppard's Jumpers: A Mystery Play." Modern Drama, 20
(1977), 87-95.

Gianakaris, C. J. "Absurdism Altered: Rosencrantz and Guildenstern Are Dead."
Drama Survey, 7, Nos. 1 and 2 (Winter 1968-69), p. 54.

Gitzen, Julian. "Tom Stoppard: Chaos in Perspective." Southern Humanities
Review, 10 (1976), 143-52.

Gold, Margaret. "Who Are the Dadas of Travesties?" Modern Drama, 21 (1978),
59-65.

Gordon, Giles. "Tom Stoppard." Transatlantic Review, 29 (1968), 17-25.

Hayman, Ronald. Tom Stoppard. Totowa, NJ: Rowman & Littlefield, 1977.

Hunter, Jim. Tom Stoppard's Plays. New York: Grove, 1982.

James, Clive. "Count Zero Splits the Infinitive: Tom Stoppard's Plays."
Encounter, 45, No. 5 (Nov. 1975), pp. 68-76.

Jensen, Henning. "Jonathan Bennett and Mr. Stoppard." Philosophy, 52 (1977), 214-17.

Kahn, Coppelia. "Travesties and the Importance of Being Stoppard." New York Literary Forum, 1 (1978), 187-97.

Leonard, Virginia E. "Tom Stoppard's Jumpers: The Separation from Reality." The Bulletin of the West Virginia Association of College English Teachers, 2 (1975), 45-56.

Londre, Felicia Hardison. Tom Stoppard. New York: Frederick Ungar, 1981.

Marowitz, Charles. "Tom Stoppard--The Theatre's Intellectual P. T. Barnum." New York Times, 19 Oct. 1975, Sec. 2, pp. 1, 5.

Pearce, Howard D. "Stage as Mirror: Tom Stoppard's Travesties." Modern Language Notes, 94 (1979), 1139-58.

Robinson, Gabriele Scott. "Plays without Plot: The Theater of Tom Stoppard." Educational Theatre Journal, 29 (1977), 37-48.

Rothstein, Bobbi. "The Reappearance of Public Man: Stoppard's Jumpers and Professional Foul." Kansas Quarterly, 12, No. 4 (1980), pp. 35-44.

Schwartzman, Myron. "Wilde about Joyce?: Da! But My Art Belongs to Dada!" James Joyce Quarterly, 13 (1975), 122-23.

Simard, Rodney. "The Logic of Unicorns: Beyond Absurdism in Stoppard." Arizona Quarterly, 38, No. 1 (Spring 1982), pp. 37-44.

Stoppard, Tom. Albert's Bridge and Other Plays. New York: Grove, 1977.

----------. "Ambushes for the Audience." Theater Quarterly, 4 (1974), 3-17.

----------. Dirty Linen and New-Found-Land. New York: Grove, 1976.

----------. Enter a Free Man. New York: Grove, 1968.

----------. Every Good Boy Deserves Favor and Professional Foul. New York: Grove, 1978.

----------. Jumpers. New York: Grove, 1972.

----------. Night and Day. New York: Grove, 1979.

----------. The Real Inspector Hound and After Magritte. New York: Grove, 1971.

----------. Rosencrantz and Guildenstern Are Dead. New York: Grove, 1967.

----------. Travesties. New York: Grove, 1975.

Tynan, Kenneth. Show People: Profiles in Entertainment. New York: Simon & Schuster, 1979.

Weightman, John. "A Metaphysical Comedy." Encounter, 38 (April 1972), 44-46.

Werner, Craig. "Stoppard's Critical Travesty, or, Who Vindicates Whom and Why." Arizona Quarterly, 35 (1979), 228-36.

Sam Shepard

Auerbach, Doris. Sam Shepard, Arthur Kopit, and the Off Broadway Theater. Boston: Twayne, 1982.

Bachman, Charles R. "Defusion of Menace in the Plays of Sam Shepard." Modern Drama, 19 (1976), 405-15.

Chubb, Kenneth. "Fruitful Difficulties of Directing Shepard." Theatre Quarterly, 4, No. 15 (Aug. 1974), pp. 17-24.

Davis, R. A. "'Get Up Out a' Your Homemade Beds': The Plays of Sam Shepard." Players, 47 (1971), 12-19.

Kelb, William. "Sam Shepard's Inacoma at the Magic Theatre." Theater, 9 (1977), 59-64.

Marranca, Bonnie, ed. American Dreams: The Imagination of Sam Shepard. New York: Performing Arts Journal Publications, 1981.

----------, and Gautam Dasgupta. American Playwrights: A Critical Survey. I. New York: Drama Book Specialists, 1981.

McCarthy, Gerry. "'Acting it out': Sam Shepard's Action." Modern Drama, 24, No. 1 (March 1981), pp. 1-12.

Oppenheim, Irene, and Victor Fascio. "The Most Promising Playwright in America Today Is Sam Shepard." Village Voice, 27 Oct. 1975, pp. 81-82.

Powe, Bruce W. "The Tooth of Crime: Sam Shepard's Way with Music." Modern Drama, 24, No. 1 (March 1981), pp. 13-25.

Rosen, Carol. "Sam Shepard's Angel City: A Movie for the Stage." Modern Drama, 22 (1979), 39-46.

Shepard, Sam. Action and the Unseen Hand. London: Faber & Faber, 1975.

----------. Angel City and Other Plays. New York: Urizen, 1976.

----------. Buried Child, Seduced, Suicide in B^b. Vancouver: Talonbooks, 1979.

----------. Chicago and Other Plays. New York: Urizen, 1967.

Shepard, Sam. Five Plays by Sam Shepard. Indianapolis: Bobbs-Merrill, 1967.

----------. Four Two-Act Plays. New York: Urizen, 1980.

----------. Mad Dog Blues and Other Plays. New York: Winter House, 1972.

----------. Seven Plays. New York: Bantam, 1981.

----------. The Unseen Hand and Other Plays. Indianapolis: Bobbs-Merrill, 1972.

Simon, John. "Theater Chronicle: Kopit, Norman, and Shepard." Hudson Review, 32
    (1979), 77-88.

Wetzsteon, Ross. "The Genius of Sam Shepard." New York, 24 Nov. 1980, pp. 20, 23,
    25.

                                   Peter Shaffer

Baldwin, Helene L. "Equus: Theater of Cruelty or Theater of Sensationalism."
    West Virginia University Philological Papers, 25 (1979), 118-27.

Buckley, Tom. "'Write Me,' Said the Play to Peter Shaffer." New York Times
    Magazine, 13 April 1975, pp. 20, 25-40.

Corbally, John. "The Equus Ethic." New Laurel Review, 7 (1977), 53-58.

Dean, Joan FitzPatrick. "Peter Shaffer's Recurrent Character Type." Modern Drama,
    21 (1978), 297-305.

Klein, Dennis A. Peter Shaffer. Boston: Twayne, 1979.

Lounsberry, Barbara. "'God-Hunting': The Chaos of Worship in Peter Shaffer's
    Equus and Royal Hunt of the Sun." Modern Drama, 21 (1978), 13-28.

Pennel, Charles A. "The Plays of Peter Shaffer: Experiment in Convention."
    Kansas Quarterly, 3 (1971), 100-09.

Plunka, Gene A. "The Existential Ritual: Peter Shaffer's Equus." Kansas
    Quarterly, 12 (1980), 87-97.

Shaffer, Peter. Amadeus. New York: Harper & Row, 1981.

----------. Equus and Shrivings. New York: Atheneum, 1976.

----------. Five Finger Exercise. New York: Harcourt, Brace, 1958.

----------. The Private Ear. New York: Samuel French, 1962.

----------. The Public Eye. New York: Samuel French, 1962.

Peter. The Royal Hunt of the Sun. New York: Ballantine, 1964.

----------. The White Liars and Black Comedy. New York: Samuel French, 1968.

Simon, John. "Hippodrama at the Psychodrome." Hudson Review, 38 (Spring 1975), 97-106.

Stacy, James R. "The Sun and the Horse: Peter Shaffer's Search for Worship." Educational Theatre Journal, 28 (Oct. 1976), 325-37.

Taylor, John Russell. Peter Shaffer. Ed. Ian Scott-Kilvert. Edinburgh: Longman, 1974.

----------. Peter Shaffer. Essex: Longman, 1976.

Timm, Neil. "Equus as a Modern Tragedy." West Virginia University Philological Papers, 25 (1979), 128-34.

Vandenbroucke, Russell. "Equus: Modern Myth in the Making." Drama and Theater, 12 (1975), 129-33.

Witham, Barry B. "The Anger in Equus." Modern Drama, 22 (1979), 61-66.

David Rabe

Asahina, Robert. "The Basic Training of American Playwrights: Theater and the Vietnam War." Theater, 9 (1978), 30-37.

Berkvist, Robert. "How Nichols and Rabe Shaped 'Streamers.'" New York Times, 25 April 1976, Sec. 2, pp. 1, 12.

Bernstein, Samuel J. The Strands Entwined: A New Direction in American Drama. Boston: Northeastern Univ. Press, 1980.

"'Boom Boom Room' and the Role of Women." New York Times, 24 Nov. 1973, p. 22.

Brown, Janet. Feminist Drama: Definition and Critical Analysis. Metuchen, NJ: Scarecrow, 1979.

Gussow, Mel. "Rabe is Compelled 'to Keep Trying.'" New York Times, 12 May 1976, p. 34.

Kerr, Walter. "David Rabe's 'House' Is Not a Home." New York Times, 2 May 1976, Sec. 2, p. 5.

Phillips, Jerrold A. "Descent Into the Abyss: The Plays of David Rabe." West Virginia University Philological Papers, 25 (Feb. 1979), 108-17.

Rabe, David. The Basic Training of Pavlo Hummel and Sticks and Bones. New York: Viking, 1973.

David. In the Boom Boom Room. New York: Knopf, 1975.

----------. The Orphan. New York: Samuel French, 1975.

----------. Streamers. New York: Knopf, 1975.

Werner, Craig. "Primal Screams and Nonsense Rhymes: David Rabe's Revolt." Educational Theatre Journal, 30 (1978), 517-29.

INDEX

Photograph by Cathy Rudnick

The Author

Rodney Simard received his PhD in Modern and Dramatic Literature from the University of Alabama in 1982. Having published a number of literary and pedagogical essays in various journals and collections, he is an Assistant Editor of The Variorum Edition of the Poetry of John Donne and a former Editor of The Black Warrior Review. Currently, he is a Lecturer in English and Communications at California State College, Bakersfield.